Table of Contents

1.1 The stages of our economy

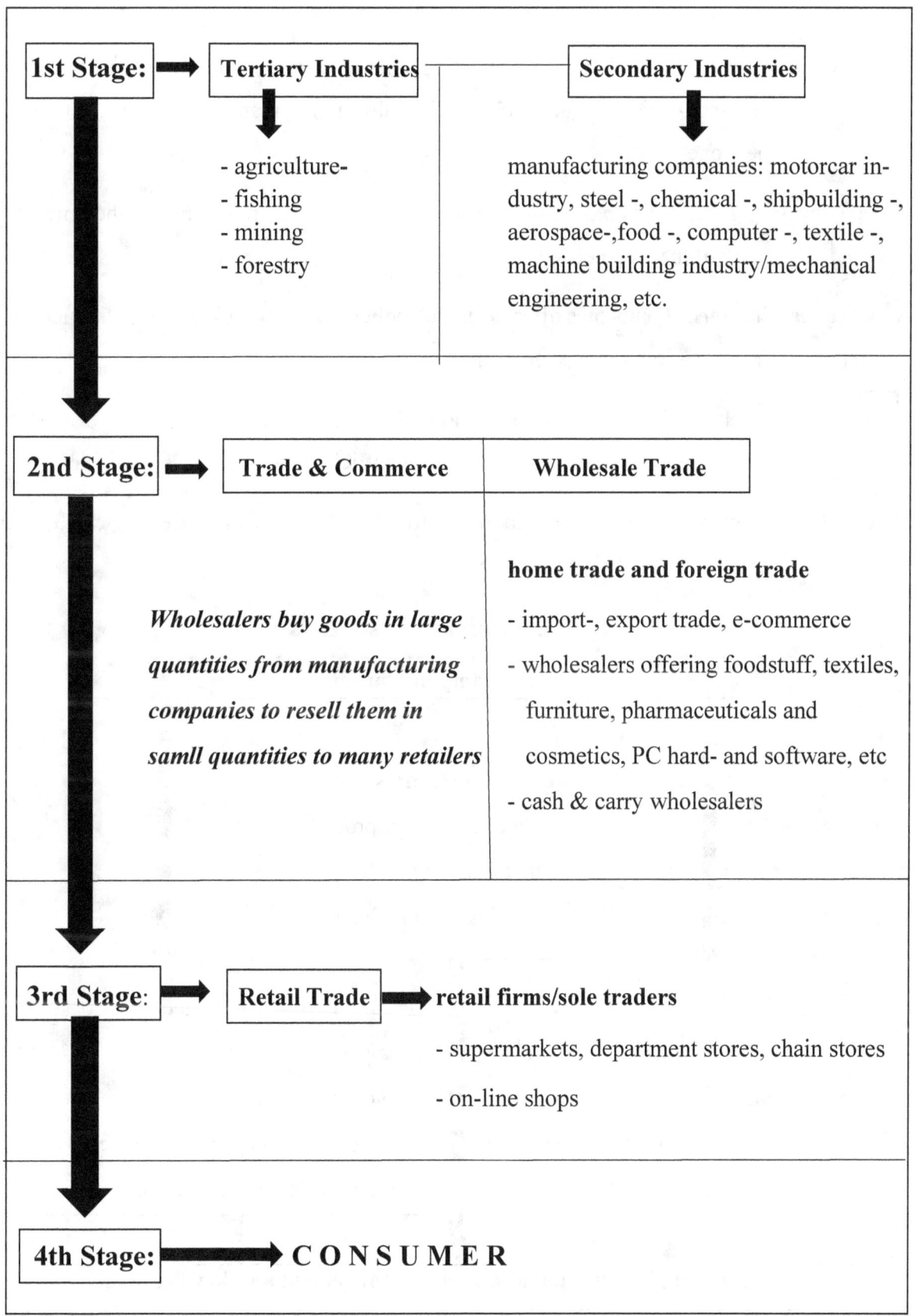

1st Stage: → **Tertiary Industries**   **Secondary Industries**

- agriculture-
- fishing
- mining
- forestry

manufacturing companies: motorcar industry, steel -, chemical -, shipbuilding -, aerospace-, food -, computer -, textile -, machine building industry/mechanical engineering, etc.

2nd Stage: → **Trade & Commerce**   **Wholesale Trade**

Wholesalers buy goods in large quantities from manufacturing companies to resell them in samll quantities to many retailers

home trade and foreign trade

- import-, export trade, e-commerce
- wholesalers offering foodstuff, textiles, furniture, pharmaceuticals and cosmetics, PC hard- and software, etc
- cash & carry wholesalers

3rd Stage: → **Retail Trade** → retail firms/sole traders

- supermarkets, department stores, chain stores
- on-line shops

4th Stage: → **C O N S U M E R**

1.2 Intermediaries/agents involved with the distribution of goods

Transport: reliable forwarding agents, shipping companies and air lines transport finished and semi-finished products by truck, train, ship or plane from one stage to the next one

Warehousing: goods are stored in warehouses to keep them secure and bridge the time until they are needed

Insurance: Insurance companies offer insurance policies aganist all kinds of risks such as loss, fire, water, breakage or theft

Banking: Banks are responsible for the smooth flow of money between suppliers and customers and also grant credits if not sufficient own capital is available

Advertising: Advertising is of vital importance to inform consumers where they can buy the products they are interested in

2. Company essentials

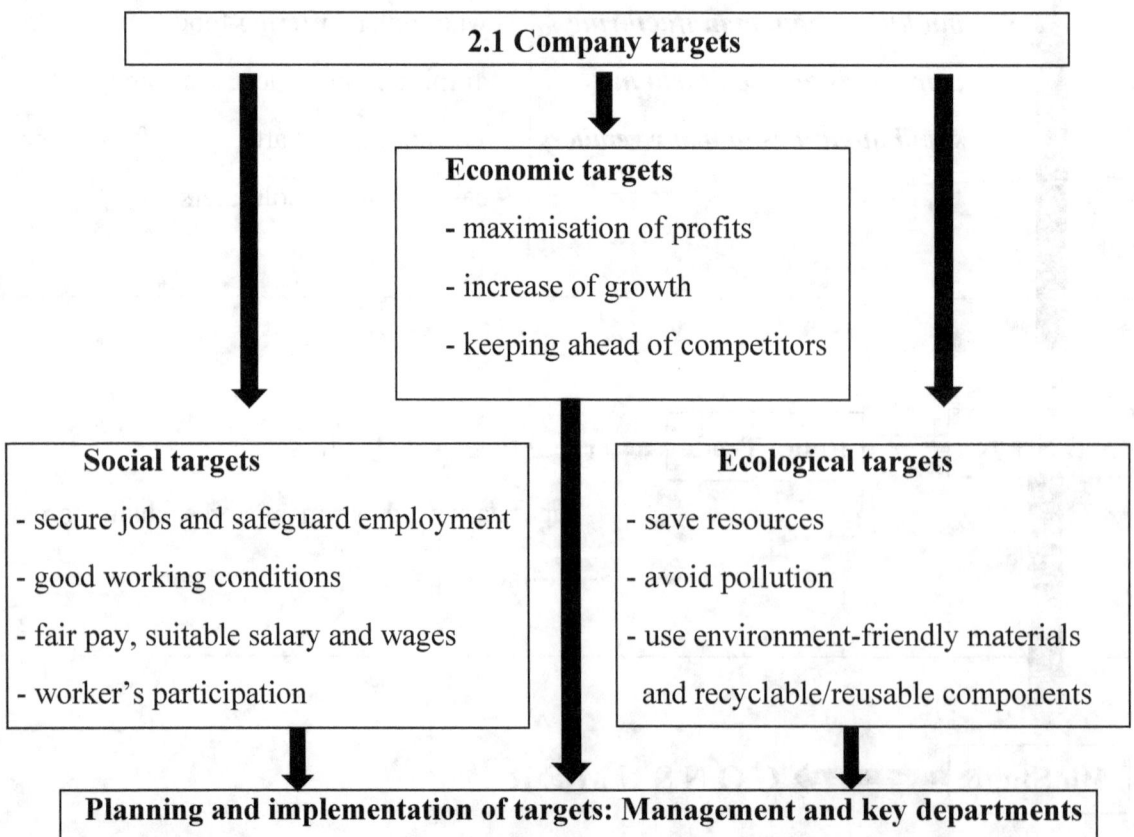

2.1 Company targets

Economic targets
- maximisation of profits
- increase of growth
- keeping ahead of competitors

Social targets
- secure jobs and safeguard employment
- good working conditions
- fair pay, suitable salary and wages
- worker's participation

Ecological targets
- save resources
- avoid pollution
- use environment-friendly materials and recyclable/reusable components

Planning and implementation of targets: Management and key departments

You should be able to talk and give detailed information about your company according to the following diagram and its keywords:

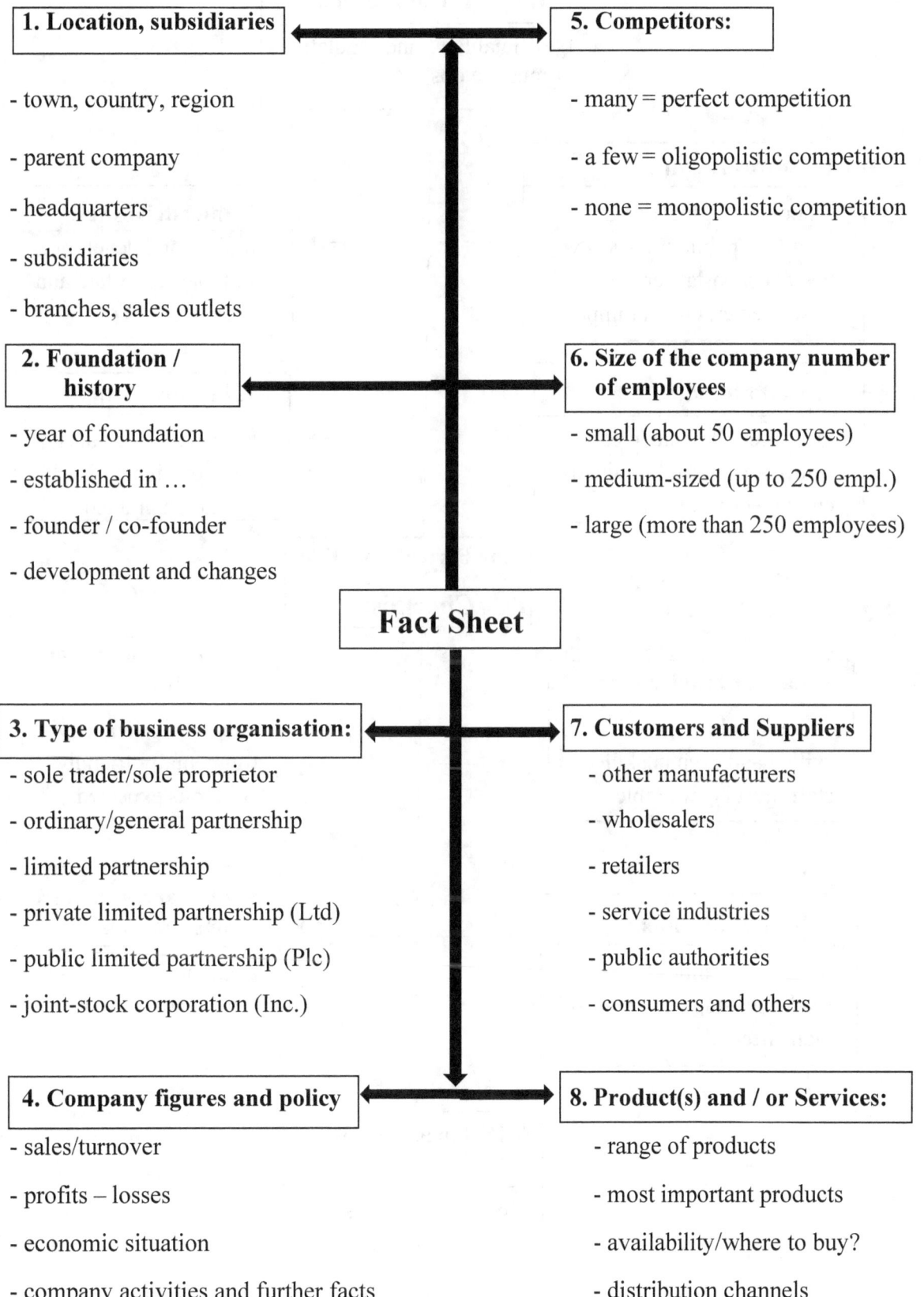

1. Location, subsidiaries

- town, country, region

- parent company

- headquarters

- subsidiaries

- branches, sales outlets

5. Competitors:

- many = perfect competition

- a few = oligopolistic competition

- none = monopolistic competition

2. Foundation / history

- year of foundation

- established in …

- founder / co-founder

- development and changes

6. Size of the company number of employees

- small (about 50 employees)

- medium-sized (up to 250 empl.)

- large (more than 250 employees)

Fact Sheet

3. Type of business organisation:

- sole trader/sole proprietor

- ordinary/general partnership

- limited partnership

- private limited partnership (Ltd)

- public limited partnership (Plc)

- joint-stock corporation (Inc.)

7. Customers and Suppliers

- other manufacturers

- wholesalers

- retailers

- service industries

- public authorities

- consumers and others

4. Company figures and policy

- sales/turnover

- profits – losses

- economic situation

- company activities and further facts

8. Product(s) and / or Services:

- range of products

- most important products

- availability/where to buy?

- distribution channels

Study the 10 factors that may be of decisive importance when you are looking for the ideal location to establish your company:

1. Legal requirements:

official laws and regulations must be observed

10. Infrastructure

schools and educational facilities, public transport, hospitals, postal services, leisure/entertainment important

2. Industrial sites:

finding and developing suitable real estate and premises

9. Staff attitudes

motivated, flexible, creative team-working and productive employees wanted

3. Financial support

tax reliefs, subsidies, generous incentives should be granted

The Perfect Location

Checklist

8. Labour requirements

skilled/qualified, semi-skilled and even unskilled staff must be available

4. Energy and water supply:

inexpensive and environmentally friendly solutions expected

7. Ideal traffic links

transport facilities by road, rail, ship and plane needed

5. Easy access to purchasing markets

availability of raw materials, components and spareparts

6. Distance to sales markets

considering relatively short distances to major customers

2.4 The company's department structure

The chart gives a survey of the company's key departments and below activities performed there:

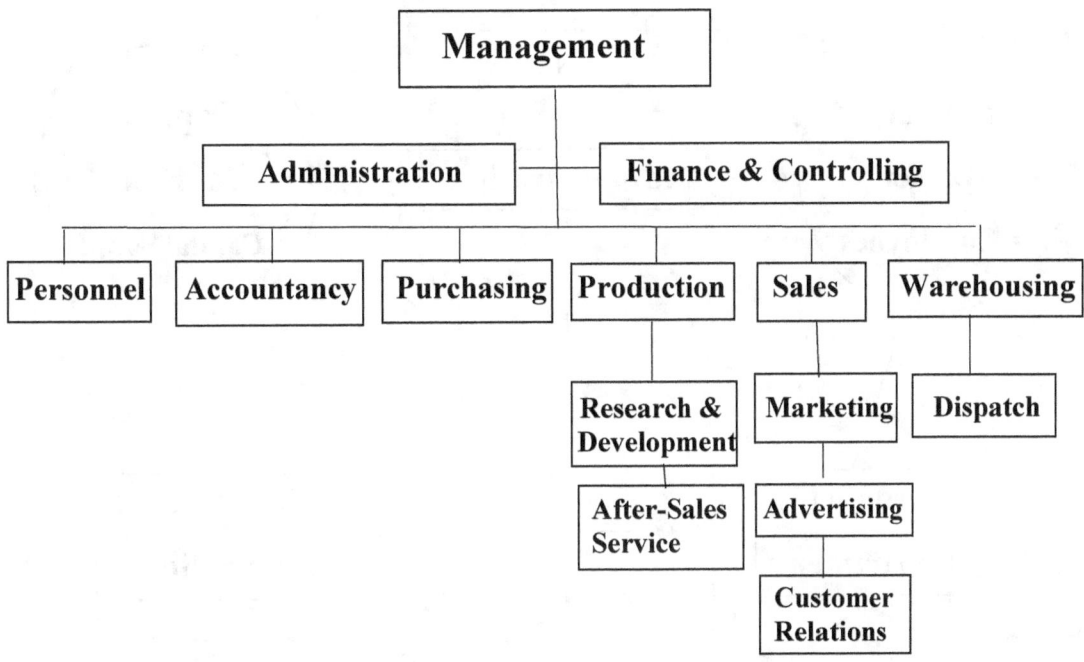

Allocate the following activities to the departments above:

1. checking consignments
2. placing orders
3. giving discounts
4. appointing a new branch manager
5. answering inquiries
6. settling invoices
7. starting advertising measures
8. informing the staff about holidays
9. receiving visitors
10. discussing new investments

11. improving products
12. stocking goods
13. getting discounts
14. hiring staff
15. having sales talks at a trade fair
16. complaining about deliveries
17. installing the new power press
18. launching commercials on TV
19. packing an airfreight consignment
20. receiving a bank transfer

2.5 Major departments and their key markets

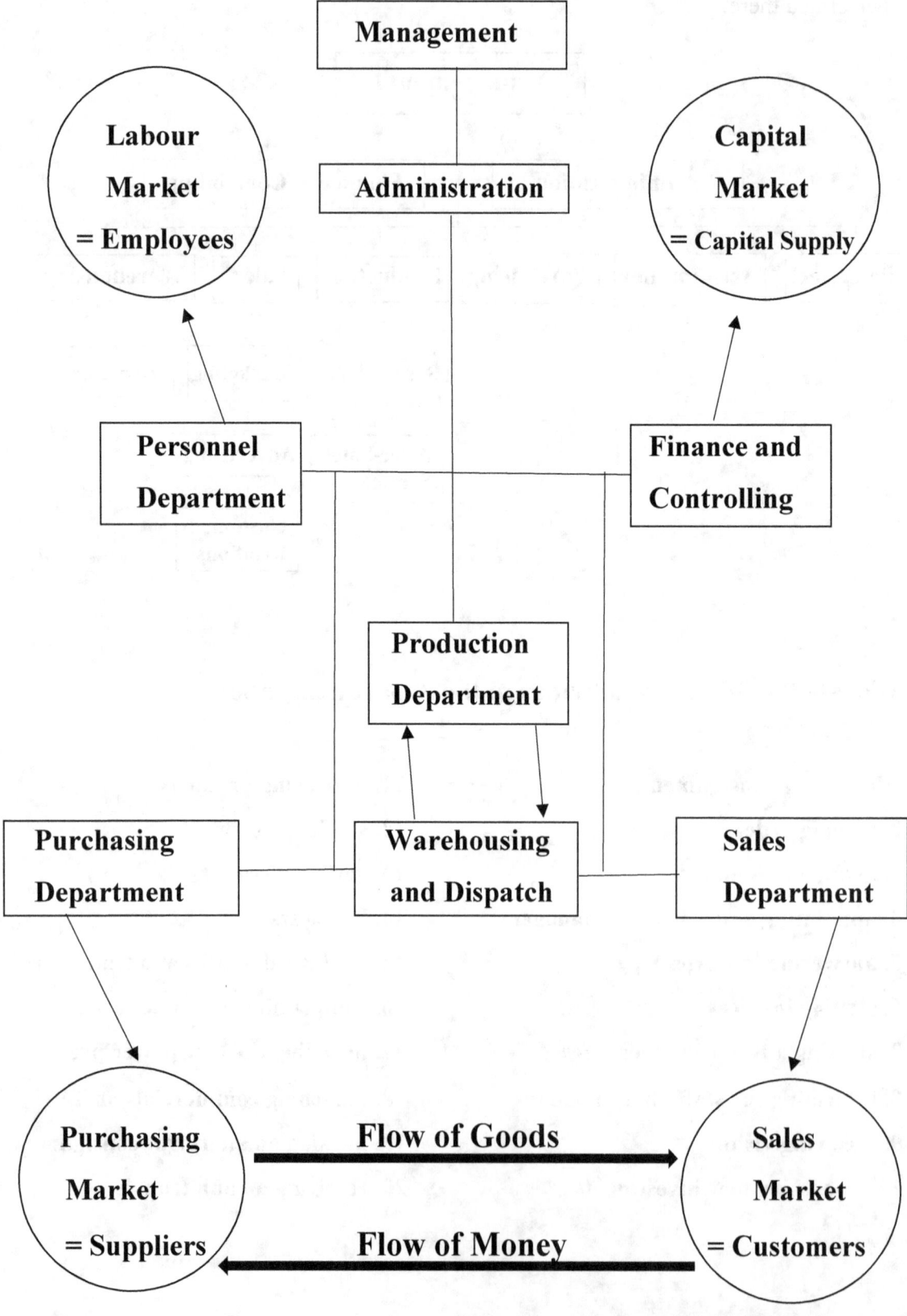

3.1 Main tasks of the purchasing department

Apart from ordering <u>goods</u> and <u>services</u> the enterprise needs, the purchasing department's tasks comprise a wide range of different activities such as:

a. observing the purchasing market to buy goods and services at the <u>right time</u>, in the <u>right quantity</u> and at <u>reasonable prices</u>.

b. keeping up business relations with reliable suppliers

c. finding more secure sources of supply on the home market and abroad

d. having negotiations with suppliers about prices and terms of business

e. typing enquiries

f. comparing incoming offers

g. placing orders

h. watching if deliveries are executed as promised

3.2 Dealing with enquiries

3.2.1 Types of enquiries/inquiries:

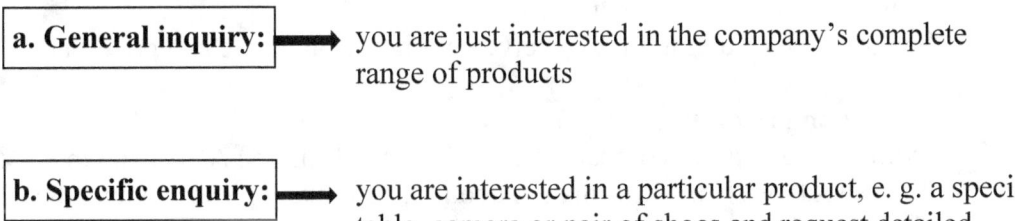

| **a. General inquiry:** | ➝ | you are just interested in the company's complete range of products |

| **b. Specific enquiry:** | ➝ | you are interested in a particular product, e. g. a specific table, camera or pair of shoes and request detailed information |

3.2.2 <u>Sources of information:</u>

a. Business organizations and local authorities: e. g. chambers of commerce, embassies, consulates

b. Advertisements in international trade papers or magazines, yellow pages, the internet

c. Mutual business partners, trade fairs and exhibitions

3.2.3 <u>Form of inquiries:</u>

Inquries may be made ...

a. in writing: by letters, faxes, E-mails

b. orally: by telephone, mobile phone, made in business meetings by sales talks

3.3 Communication in the purchasing department:
- Phrases commonly used in inquiries -

Introduction:
- We refer to your advertisement/circular/e-mail
- We have been referred to you by ....
- We owe your address to ....
- As we have learned from ...you are producer of ...
- We have seen your advertisement in ...
- During a visit at your stand at the Cebit

Reasons for enquiry:
- We are interested in ...
- We are in the market for ...
- As our stock is running low ...
- As we have to replenish our stock ...

Requests for information
- Please inform us about/concerning...
- Please let us know ...
- We should appreciate detailed information
- We should be pleased to receive ...
- Please quote/state your lowest/keenest/best/most favourable prices ...
- Let us have your earliest delivery date
- We should be glad/grateful to receive your latest catalogue and price-list

Giving references:
- Information about our company can be obtained from the ABC bank in XYZ.
- If you should wish any information about our company please contact the Chamber of Commerce in XYZ.

Business prospects:
- If your prices are competitive/favourable ...
- If your products come up to/meet our expectations, you may count on big orders.
- If the samples meet our requirements, we will place a trial order.

Closing phrases:
- Please send/submit us your offer/quotation as soon as possible.
- We hope to receive your answer/reply/Email by return.
- We look forward to receiving your answer within the next few days.

3.3.1 Writing an enquiry: E-mail / Letter Writing

Write an inquiry for your company Parker & Sons, 86 Bradford Road, Birmingham BR4 2HM to the Swedish manufacturer Berglund & Lindgren AB,12 – 14 Kungsgatan, 11152 Stockholm, to receive further information about their smoke-alarm sets. Please use the following notes:

- information from the internet
- the Swedish firm produces security system
- introduce your company: medium-sized wholesaler
                               supplier of Do-It-Yourself retail shops
- interested in smoke-alarm sets "Nordic Fire Fighter"
- information about Parker & Sons : from Chamber of Commerce, Birmingham

ask for:
- illustrated sales literature
- favourable prices important because of keen competition
- any price reductions
- reasonable terms of delivery and payment
- short delivery times
- immediate reply

3.3.2 Writing an enquiry: E-mail / Letter Writing

Write an enquiry to: East West Fashion Ltd., New Upper Link Road 26, Dhaka 1000, Bangladesh. You work for Top Fashion, Via Loano 68, Rome.

- refer to mutual business partner and fashion week in Paris
- interest in whole range of products
- introduce your firm: leading import agent, specialized in buying textiles
                         customers: big mail-order houses and department stores

ask for:
- latest catalogues
- terms of sale
- prices, including introductory and quantity discounts
- customized production possibilities: to react to market demands
- sample T-shirts and sweaters for test purposes
- you may place trial order provided quality and design are o.k.
- information about TOP Fashion can be received from XYZ Bank in Milano
- if products sell well repeat orders may follow
- hope to get answer within the next few days
- look forward to establishing business relations with East-West Fashion

4. The sales department

4.1. Main tasks of the sales department

The sales department is another key department of an enterprise which is very interested in increasing the company's profits and strongly co-operates with the departments of marketing, advertising and customer service. Major activities are as follows:

a. checking and answering enquiries

b. submitting offers

c. receiving orders

d. confirming orders

e. caring about customer problems

f. optimising marketing activities

g. launching advertising campaigns

h. streamlining the distribution of goods

4.2 How sales contracts are concluded

The four steps show the willingness of the trading parties to buy respectively to sell a commodity on the terms stipulated:

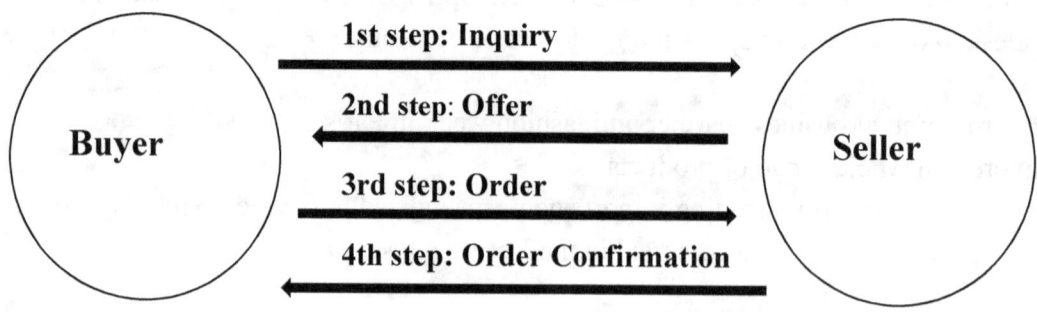

11. Dealing with offers

4.2.1 Types of offers:

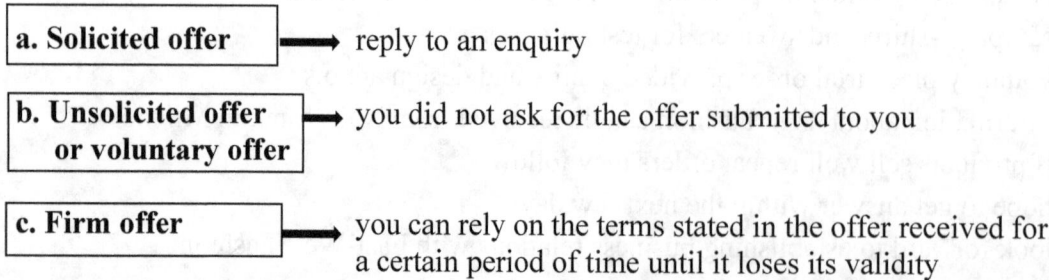

d. Claused offer → certain clauses/statements in the offer indicate that the supplier is not bound to it forever. You may find such clauses as follows:
- This offer is given without engagement.
- Prices are subject to change without notice.

e. Counter offer → the initial offer is not accepted. You make clear, however, that you are willing to accept it if the terms in certain points can be improved, e. g. by getting better prices or terms of payment and delivery.

4.2.2 Contents of offers:

a. Nature of product → type, quality, article no., colour or size, etc.

b. Quantity → units, items, kilos, metres, bottles or litres, etc.

c. Prices and price reductions → as per quantity offered

→ - quantity discount
- introductory discount
- first/initial order discount
- trade discount

d. Terms of delivery → **INCOTERMS**

EXW = Ex Works, ex warehouse (... named place)
FCA = Free Carrier (... named place)
CPT = Carriage Paid To (... named place of destination)
CIP = Carriage Insurance Paid to (... named place of destination)
DAT = Delivered At Terminal (... named place or terminal)
DAP = Delivered At Place (... named place)
DDP = Delivered Duty Paid (... named place of destination)

For sea and inland waterway transport:

FAS = Free Alongside Ship (... named port of loading)
FOB = Free On Board (... named port of loading)
CFR = Cost & Freight (... named port of destination)
CIF = Cost, Insurance, Freight (... named port of destination)

Questions on Incoterms:

a. Give the best Incoterm for the seller.
b. State the best Incoterm for the buyer.
c. What is the difference between FAS and FOB?
d. Why is the term CIP better than CPT for the buyer?
e. Why should fragile or valuable goods not shipped on a CFR basis?

e. Time of delivery 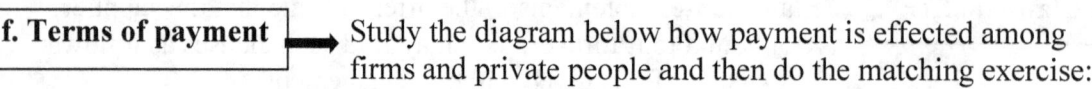 as confirmed between buyer and seller

f. Terms of payment Study the diagram below how payment is effected among firms and private people and then do the matching exercise:

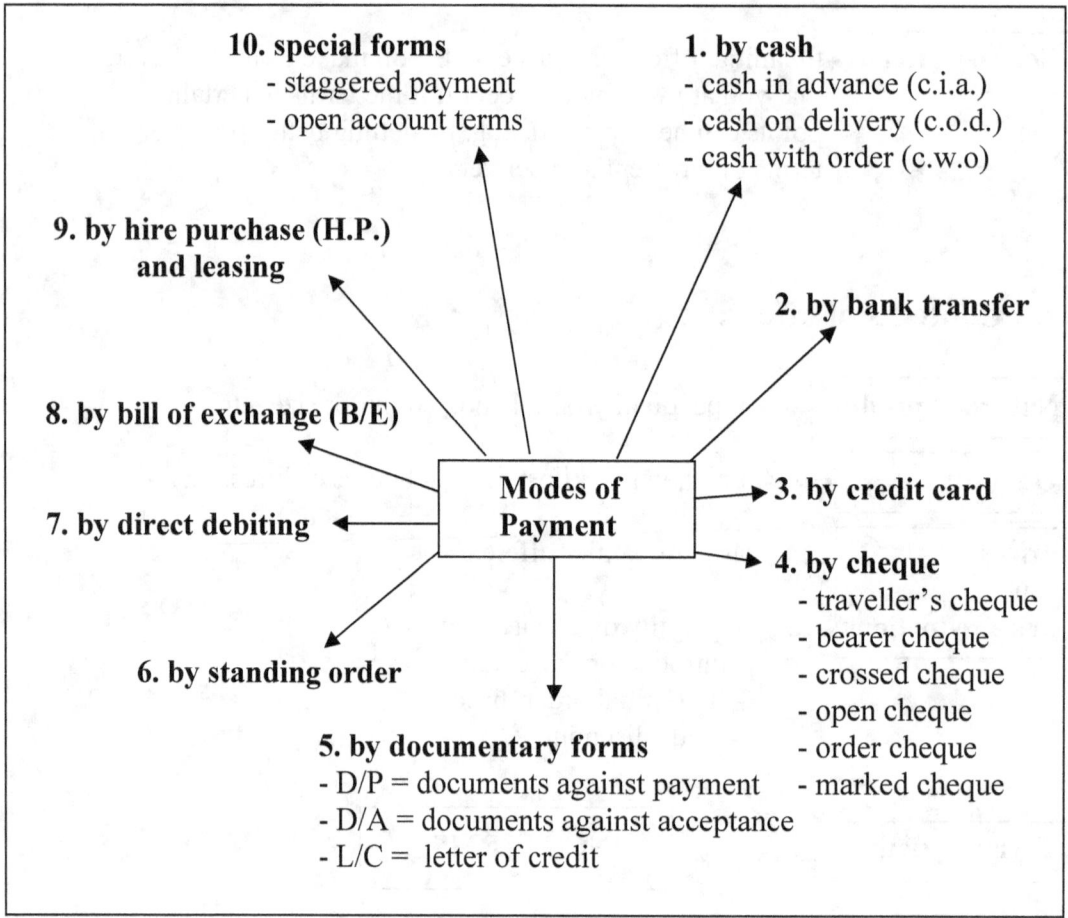

10. special forms
- staggered payment
- open account terms

1. by cash
- cash in advance (c.i.a.)
- cash on delivery (c.o.d.)
- cash with order (c.w.o)

9. by hire purchase (H.P.) and leasing

2. by bank transfer

8. by bill of exchange (B/E)

7. by direct debiting

Modes of Payment

3. by credit card

4. by cheque
- traveller's cheque
- bearer cheque
- crossed cheque
- open cheque
- order cheque
- marked cheque

6. by standing order

5. by documentary forms
- D/P = documents against payment
- D/A = documents against acceptance
- L/C = letter of credit

Matching modes of payment:

a. You want to buy something very expensive so that your cheque needs a confirmation of your bank which says that you have sufficient capital.

b. Your debt is repaid in monthly instalments

c. You have signed the paper and accepted to pay the debt within 30, 60 or 90 days.

d. It is the safest method of payment in foreign trade as banks guarantee payment.

e. You regularly place big orders with your supplier who expects payment every two months.

f. Once a month the same amount is paid by your bank for the rent of your flat.

g. After the buyer in the importing country has paid the invoice amount he will get the documents for the release of the goods.

h. Your bills for electricity and your mobile are automatically paid by your bank every month.

i. As the invoice amount is much too high the buyer and seller have agreed to pay 1/3 of the total amount with receipt of order, 1/3 when the goods are delivered and 1/3 within 30 days after date of invoice.

j. Everybody who presents this cheque will get the money.

k. You can't cash the amount of the cheque, which is crossed with two parallel lines, as it is credited to your current account.

4.3 Communication in the sales department:
- Phrases commonly used in offers -

Introduction:
- We refer to your enquiry / e-mail / phone call of … and are pleased
  to quote as follows
- As requested / desired, we are sending you …. enclosed.
- We thank you for your letter of September 23 and are glad to submit
  our latest price-list as requested
- We have learned from your enquiry that you are interested in our range of
  products / latest catalogue / sales literature.

Prices and discounts:
- Our prices are net cash / are to be understood net cash
- A quantity discount of … % can be granted on orders exceeding 500 units
- We allow / grant a price reduction /a deduction / a trade discount of … %
- We offer an introductory discount of … % on first orders
- The price quoted is ex works / CIF London / FOB Tokyo

Payment:
- Payment has to be effected by cash in advance / cash with order (CWO) /
  cash on delivery (COD)
- Payment is to be made by bank transfer within 10 days after date of invoice
  less 2 % cash discount or within 30 days after date of invoice net cash
- Payment has to be arranged by irrevocable and confirmed letter of credit (LC)
- Payment is to be made by documents against payment (DP)

Delivery:
- Delivery will be executed by ship as soon as possible.
- Despatch will be arranged by airfreight immediately.
- Delivery will be carried out by lorry within two weeks after receipt of order.

Validity:
- This offer is only firm/valid until …. June 22
- Our offer is given without engagement
- Our prices are subject to change without notice

Closing phrases:
- We hope our offer will come up to your expectations / requirements.
- We assure you that your order will be executed promptly and carefully.
- We will do our very best to carry out your order to your complete satisfaction.
- We look forward to receiving your order in the near future.

4.3.1 Writing an offer: E-mail / Letter Writing

Your company MCO China Tech Co. Ltd, 48 Shun Tung Rd., Hong Kong, has received an enquiry for power tools from: Ron Hobson & Co., 75 White Lane, Sydney/Australia. Please write an offer for your boss on the notes given to you. Use today's date.

- thank for general enquiry of 21 of last month for power tools

- refer to excellent reputation of your products

- enclose illustrated catalogue and latest price list

- quote prices EXW Hong Kong

- large orders may be delivered on a FOB or even CIF basis

- say to be prepared to offer special discounts; dependent on size of order

- terms of payment:first order = against irrevocable and confirmed letter of credit

- repeat orders by bank transfer within 30 days after date of invoice net cash <u>or:</u> within 2 weeks after date of invoice less 2 % cash discount

- delivery time: generally 3 weeks after receipt of order

- hope offer meets expectations and look forward to doing business with Hobson

4.3.2 Writing an offer: E-mail / Letter Writing

Toronto Machines Ltd has received an enquiry from Dubois & Monnier S.A., 26 Rue de Rennes, 72000 Le Mans. Please reply to their enquiry by using the following notes in your offer. Use today's date.

- thank for today's enquiry and interest in company's chain saw "Professional"

- latest development of completely fully automatic generation

- offer at unit price Can$ 36,50

- volume of order less than Can$ 2000,00 delivery ex works

- substantial order willing to grant quantity discount of 10 % and trading discount of 15 %

- terms of payment: documents against payment; later more favourable terms
   may be granted

- delivery: at present 2 months after receipt of order, despatch: container transport to Le Havre

- validity of offer: 3 weeks; recommend to accept offer soon; price increases expected

- further information: www.torontomach.com

- look forward to getting order, promise prompt and careful execution of indent

4.3.3 Counter-offer: E-mail / Letter Writing:

As Midland Furniture Ltd. is not satisfied with the offer you submitted, your company W. Lange & Co. in Zuerich/Switzerland has received the following e-mail.

e-mail		
From:	John Anderson, Midland Furniture	cc:
To:	stefan.kerner.@wlange.ch	
Subject:	table milling-machines	
Attachment		

Dear Mr Kerner,

We thank you for your offer of 5th of this month concerning your table milling-machines, type WM/XR 465. We are sorry to say that the unit price of € 385, 60 stated in your export price-list has not met our expectations as you did not grant any price reduction.

Apart from this, we are dissatisfied with the extremely long delivery time of six weeks after receipt of order.

As you may know yourself competing Asian companies offer their products at more favourable terms. Will you please be so kind to improve your offer and check if you can accommodate us as far as your prices and delivery dates are concerned.

We look forward to hearing from you as soon as possible.

Kind regards
John Anderson
Midland Furniture
129 Birmingham Lane
Leeds LE2 4DS
Phone: 33671-4235609
Fax: 33671-4235610
e-mail: john.anderson@midlandfurniture.co/uk

Reply to the above e-mail:

Read the preceding E-mail carefully and write your reply to Midland Furniture by using the notes given to you.

- thank for yesterday's E-mail

- feel sorry you can't reduce basic price

- reasons: first-class quality, efficiency, high safety standards

- product was tested better than most rival products in magazine "At Work"

- you are willing to grant introductory discount of 8 %

- also offer additional quantity discount of 10 % if more than 10 items are ordered

- quote CIF instead of CFR

- agree to shorten delivery time by 2 weeks when part delivery is o.k.

- terms of payment cannot be changed and remain 30 days after date of invoice net cash.

- phone call or email expected if further questions

From:		cc:
To:		
Subject:		
Attachment		

Text ......

5. Dealing with orders

5.1 The importance of orders for the company's targets

The far-reaching economic importance of orders and the wide variety of company targets affected

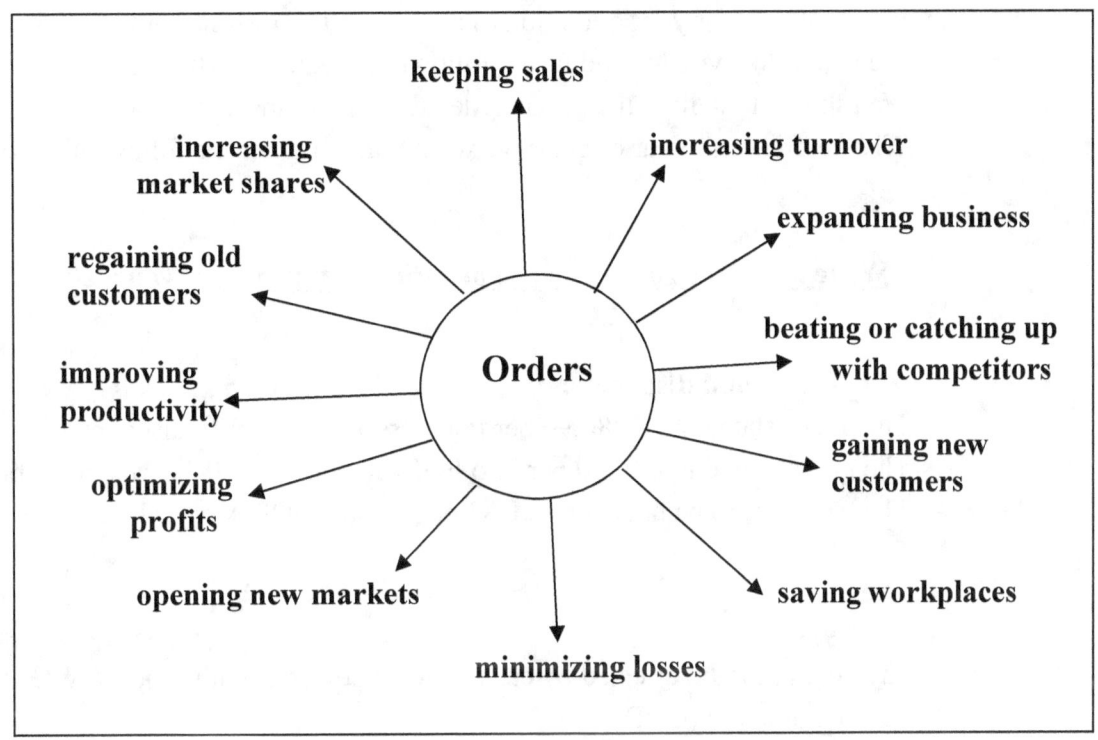

5.2 Contents of orders:

normally orders should be in accordance with the offer made by the supplier and mainly contain:

1. Supplier's name and address

2. Customer's name and address

3. Order number and date

4. Article number

5. Description of the goods

6. Quantity of units ordered

7. Unit price

8. Value/total price of items

9. Discounts

10. Insurance

11. Packing costs

12. Value Added Tax (VAT)

13. Total invoice amount

5.3 Ordering goods or services

Introduction:
- We refer to your offer / Email / phone call of … and are pleased
  to place our order no. 231/4 on the terms stated below:
- We thank you for your quotation / letter dated 14th of last month.
- We would like you to send us the following products / articles:
- We ask you to deliver the goods ordered on the terms as follows:
- With reference to your circular we would like to order the following articles:

Write down the goods you are ordering in this part of your letter

Prices and discounts:
- The prices stated are € 286,90 per item less 10 % quantity discount
- The price quoted is $ 40,30 per kilo FOB Boston, less 10 % price reduction
- The terms are to be understood £ 83.60 per unit DDP Amsterdam.

Payment:
- Payment has to be effected by cash in advance / cash with order (CWO) /
  cash on delivery (COD)
- Payment is to be made by bank transfer within 10 days after date of invoice
  less 2 % cash discount or within 30 days after date of invoice net cash
- Payment has to be arranged by irrevocable and confirmed letter of credit (LC)
- Payment is to be made by documents against payment (DP)

Delivery:
- Delivery will be executed by parcel post as soon as possible.
- Despatch will be arranged by airfreight / ship / rail immediately.
- Delivery will be carried out by lorry within two weeks after receipt of order.

Closing phrases:
- We hope that you will give this indent your prompt attention..
- We trust that you will execute our order promptly and carefully.
- We look forward to receiving your order confirmation by return and hope
  you will carry out our order to our complete satisfaction.

You work for: Manchester Engineering Ltd, 84 Morgan Road, Manchester MA2 4TR, Great Britain. Today your company places an order with ScanSteel SA, 130 Lindbergs Gata, 11825 Stockholm. Please write a stylish business letter / Email on the following notes:

- refer to sales talk at "Metal Fair "in Leeds and the offer submitted to you
- Order as follows:

200 stainless steel chains, article no. 71.5
    unit price SKR 37,90

300 carbon steel bars, article no. 93.8
    unit price SKR 24,60

- as regular customer 10 % quantity discount on both products
- steel qualities according to test reports and in accordance with QSC certificates
- prices stated above CPT Manchester
- payment: by bank transfer 30 days after date of invoice net cash
- delivery: 50 items each, part delivery by airfreight within two weeks after receipt of order
- the remaining quantity by lorry four weeks after receipt of order at the latest,
- propose to use forwarding agency TransEuro, very reliable forwarder
- expect careful execution of order

5.3.2 Writing an order: E-mail / Letter Writing

Write an order for your employer W. Van Kerkhof & Co., 83 Utrechtstraat, NL - 1074BK Amsterdam on the notes your boss has given to you. You supplier is: John Hinkley & Co. 92 Sussex Ring, Margate MR5 3AT, Great Britain. Please use today's date.

- thank for offer of 3rd of last month
- place order for 10 power tools, article no. 34.7
- first small trial order; you have not done business with the company
- unit price £ 76.40 CPT Amsterdam, less 10 % introductory discount.
- payment: by bank transfer after 30 days date of invoice net cash or within 2 weeks
  less 2 % cash discount
- delivery: within 10 days after receipt of order; as urgent order delivery time must be kept
  and any delay avoided
- despatch: as agreed on phone call by freight forwarder "Speed & More" via Rotterdam to
  Van Kerkof's Amsterdam warehouses
- when goods meet expectations and sell well on Dutch market regular and more substantial
  orders may follow
- trust that order carried out to utmost satisfaction, hope to establish good business relations

6. Marketing

6.1 Marketing-Mix Instruments

6.2 The 4 Ps of Marketing

The 4 Ps stand for: <u>P</u>roduct - <u>P</u>rice - <u>P</u>lace – <u>P</u>romotion

a. Product policy: ⟶ decisions are taken about a particular product or the complete range of products the company wants to sell to individual target groups, including design, quality, size, colour, weight and packaging

b. Pricing policy: ⟶ finding the "best" price to offer your product/service on the market such as unit prices, introductory and special prices, price reductions, quantity discounts, cash discounts, terms of delivery, Incoterms

c. Place: ⟶ thinking about places where to sell to/buy your products: manufacturing companies, wholesalers, retailers, department stores, mail-order houses, chain stores and how to get your products to these customers which means that smooth distribution channels should be available.

d. Promotion: ⟶ refers to all the activities to inform the public about your product by advertisements in newspapers and magazines, on the radio or on TV, by sales letters and circulars, catalogues, leaflets, flyers, brochures, fairs or sales promotion campaigns by presenting your product and showing how it works also on the Internet

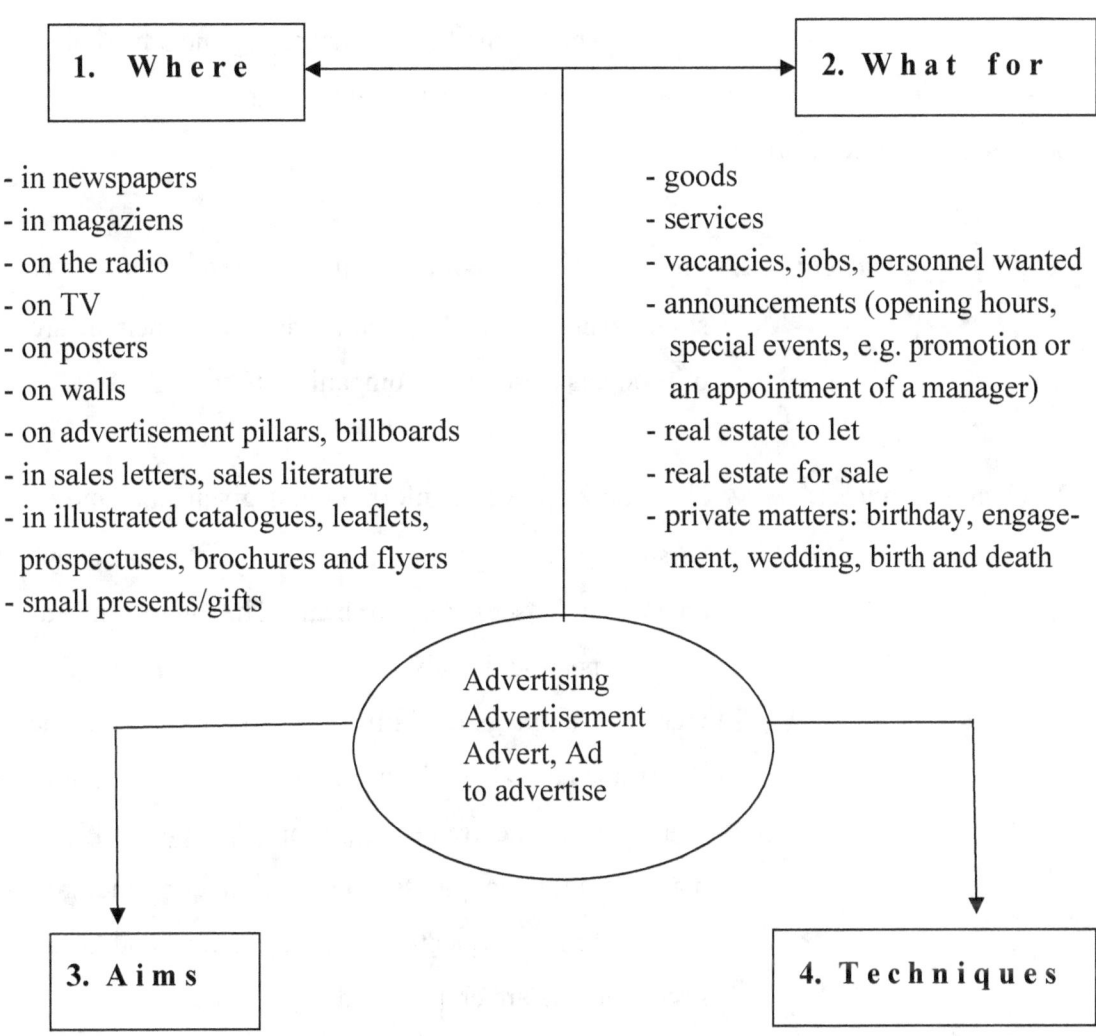

1. Where

- in newspapers
- in magaziens
- on the radio
- on TV
- on posters
- on walls
- on advertisement pillars, billboards
- in sales letters, sales literature
- in illustrated catalogues, leaflets,
  prospectuses, brochures and flyers
- small presents/gifts

2. What for

- goods
- services
- vacancies, jobs, personnel wanted
- announcements (opening hours,
  special events, e.g. promotion or
  an appointment of a manager)
- real estate to let
- real estate for sale
- private matters: birthday, engagement, wedding, birth and death

Advertising
Advertisement
Advert, Ad
to advertise

3. Aims

- to inform the public, potential
  consumers

- to influence people

- to make people buy something

- to increase or at least stabilize
  the company's sales/turnover

- to react towards competition/
  competitors

4. Techniques

- to repeat a slogan, certain words
  or phrases to memorize them
- to show the good side of life: at-
  tractive girls/boys, rich people,
  wonderful places/landscape
- use of scientific language/words
  to impress people
- cause a bad conscience and guilt
  feelings
- to establish a brand name
- use of key words: young, intelli-
  gent, golden, unbeatable
- before and after method (before
  and after using a certain product to
  show differences)

6.3.1 Advertising and the AIDA – Formula

The AIDA principle is of great importance in the field of marketing and advertising to achieve the company's main targets to increase sales and profits as much as possible. The model works in four steps as follows:

1st step = | **Attention:** | ⟶ First of all it is important to attract the attention of customers and potential customers and make them aware of products or services companies are trying to sell.

2nd step = | **Interest:** | ⟶ Now more appealing information is given and a more persuasive language is used to convince the consumer about what he sees, reads or hears. The interest increases by repeating the advantages of the product or service. The language used differs a lot between consumer goods and capital goods, e.g. a machine. On the one hand you can find an extremely emotional language which may stress fun, happiness, comfort with consumer goods, whereas rational aspects such as cost, time, and labour saving effects are emphasized with a machine.

3rd step = | **Desire:** | ⟶ After all you will be convinced of the commodity and feel you must have it. The promising and claiming information as well as the colourful photos are too strong to resist any longer. Apart from this famous people are shown who also use the product. Additionally you may be encouraged by getting small gifts, prizes and rewards in case you decide to buy.

4th step = | **Action:** | ⟶ People are taking action now on their desire and take the final step by purchasing the product or service. At this point the marketing and advertising experts have reached their goal and successfully completed their campaign.

6.4 Fairs and Exhibitions

Fairs and exhibitions are the ideal meeting place for manufacturers and customers to talk, do business with each other, to compare competing products, watch rival companies and the latest market trends.

Throughout the year a large number of trade fairs are organised, so that it is not easy to find the right fair, at the right place and a suitable date among the numerous events. Worldwide trade fairs have specialised and concentrated on the goods or services of their exhibitors. Some well-know trade fairs deal with:

- Building and Construction
- Health and Medicine
- Food and Beverage
- Metalworking

- Fashion and Textiles
- Motorshow
- Information Technologies
- Logistics and Transport

It may be a rewarding activity for exhibitors to take part in trade fairs, if considering that the leading industrial show had 6,500 international exhibitors, 200,000 visitors and 5,600,000 business contacts.

6.4.1 Check-up: planning participation at a trade fair

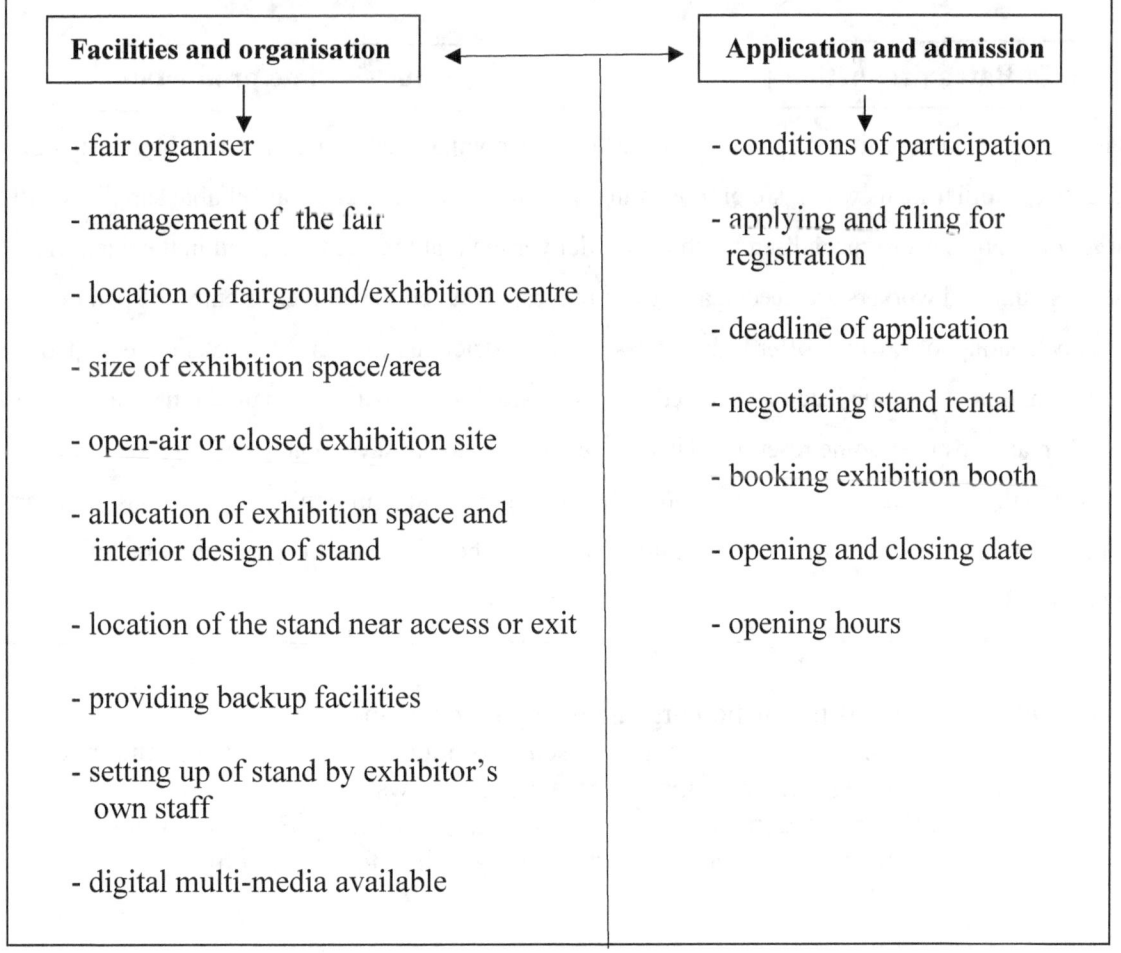

Facilities and organisation	Application and admission
- fair organiser	- conditions of participation
- management of the fair	- applying and filing for registration
- location of fairground/exhibition centre	- deadline of application
- size of exhibition space/area	- negotiating stand rental
- open-air or closed exhibition site	- booking exhibition booth
- allocation of exhibition space and interior design of stand	- opening and closing date
- location of the stand near access or exit	- opening hours
- providing backup facilities	
- setting up of stand by exhibitor's own staff	
- digital multi-media available	

7. Production

7.1 Comparing production methods

1. Job production

The production of a unique product which is made according to a specific plan or drawing e.g. your bungalow or racing boat, is called job production. The final product is rather expensive as it is manufactured by qualified employees, who in many cases, also use expensive materials. It often takes weeks or months to get the finished article.

3. Mass -, flow- or large-scale production

Mass production means to produce identical articles of a standard quality in very high quantities which help to reduce the costs per unit. You will see many low-skilled workers on assembly lines performing repetitive tasks. Before starting mass production the company must invest large sums of money which are spent on assembly lines and high-tech machinery. As a result, breakdowns cause big problems.

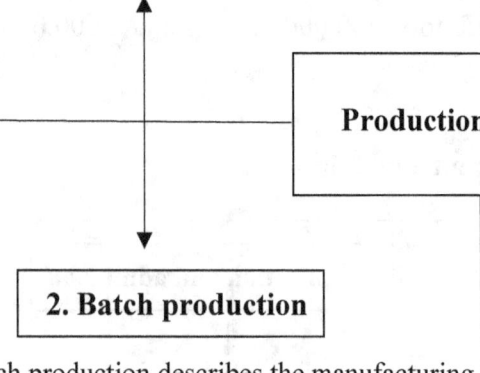

Production Methods

2. Batch production

Batch production describes the manufacturing process of similar items which are produced in larger quantities. More specialised machinery, but less qualified workers are needed as they often do routine jobs, which offer little job satisfaction. Sometimes the batch is changed and certain machines need some resetting. This is done in the car industry when a new model with 2, 4 or 5 doors or with 4 and 6 cylindres is produced.

4. Just-in-time production

When a company uses just-in-time (JIT), it can optimize the flow of materials as reliable suppliers will deliver them at the right time and in the quantities requested. When the deliveries enter the plant there will be strict quality control checks to keep quality standards. As the parts are manufactured elsewhere the producer can save money and also keep warehousing costs at a minimum, whereas business partners may benefit from this particular kind of lean production.

Questions:
1. How is production organized in your company?
2. What kind of production is used to produce: T-shirts, a swimming pool, pens, escalators, copy paper, a plane, screws or shoes.
3. Refer to companies you know and say how they produce their goods.
4. Which kind of factory work would you like to do and why?

7.2 Pros and Cons of Mass Production

PROS	CONS
- technological progress supports efficiency - increases in production - high wages - low costs - low prices of mass-produced articles - high productivity - same quality all the time - machines do not get tired, angry or frustrated - improvements of working conditions, e.g. more leisure, extra pay, social benefits, vouchers to obtain canteen meals free of charge, health and sport activities offered by the firm.	- monotonous and boring work offering little scope for personal development - negative attitude towards the job: effects = poor morale, high absenteeism - lack of know-how as traditional skills of the workers will disappear - danger of monopolistic companies which can dictate prices and sales conditions - health problems: people get ill by shift work (three-shift system) - companies move production to low-wage countries (= outsourcing)

7.3 Developing new products

When a product has gone through the four phases of the product life cycle **a. introduction, b. growth, c. maturity** and **d. decline**, it must be replaced by a new product, which principally has to pass the following stages:

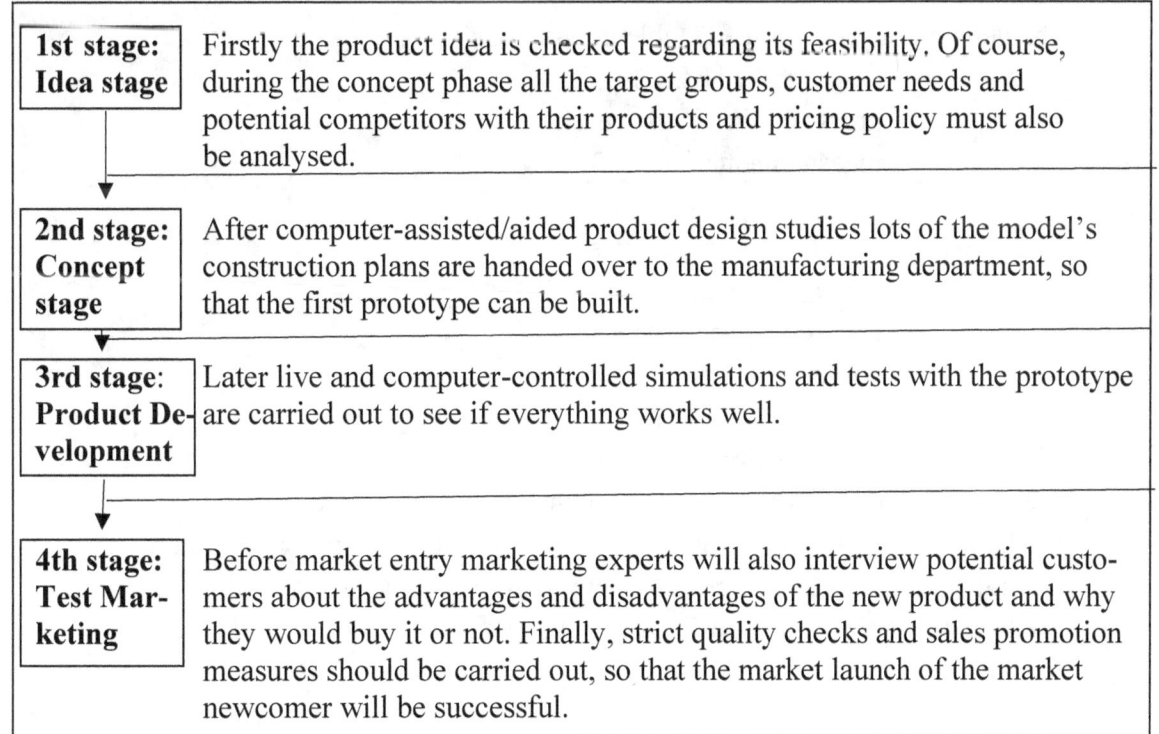

1st stage: Idea stage	Firstly the product idea is checked regarding its feasibility. Of course, during the concept phase all the target groups, customer needs and potential competitors with their products and pricing policy must also be analysed.
2nd stage: Concept stage	After computer-assisted/aided product design studies lots of the model's construction plans are handed over to the manufacturing department, so that the first prototype can be built.
3rd stage: Product Development	Later live and computer-controlled simulations and tests with the prototype are carried out to see if everything works well.
4th stage: Test Marketing	Before market entry marketing experts will also interview potential customers about the advantages and disadvantages of the new product and why they would buy it or not. Finally, strict quality checks and sales promotion measures should be carried out, so that the market launch of the market newcomer will be successful.

8. The Dispatch of goods

8.1 Communication regarding dispatch matters
- Phrases commonly used in this context -

Introduction:
- We are pleased to inform you that your goods were sent by rail today.
- We are writing to tell you that your spare parts will be delivered by lorry tomorrow.
- We have pleasure in telling you that your order no. 757/9 of July 26th regarding high-speed motor pumps is ready for dispatch.
- We hereby inform you that the consignment containing your tools will be dispatched this afternoon.

Dispatch particulars:
- The consignment will be collected by the freight forwarder/forwarding agency/haulage company *TDUP* tomorrow morning.
- Our company will arrange dispatch of your goods by *German Rail* to Rotterdam-*Europort* today.
- We have booked the shipping space on board **MS Global Seas** which will leave / which is due to leave Le Havre for Montevideo on September 23rd.
- We handed over your consignment to our shipping agency *BLUE OCEAN,* which will pass on your goods in accordance to your shipping instructions.
- Your consignment will be shipped by *Japan Airlines* from Copenhagen to Osaka via Abu Dhabi on flight no. 745, air waybill no. JA 745/359.

Details on consignments:
- The delivery of your 120 LED table lamps consists of:
        3 cases marked SLK 1 – 3
            gross weight 32 kilos each
            measurements 4 x 3 x 3 feet

- As agreed, you will receive as follows:
            1 container, marking UCL/16
            60 bikes, type: winner
            colour: red, frame size 52

Closing phrases:
- We trust that the delivery will arrive in time and good condition.
- We hope that the goods will arrive without any delay and in perfect condition.
- We hope to receive further orders from you soon / in the near future.
- We look forward to doing business with you again.

8.1.1 Writing an advice of dispatch: E-mail / Letter Writing

Write the following advice of dispatch on behalf of your company H. Klein KG,
47 Hauptstr., 80403 München to: Henry S. Morgan & Co., 36 - 39 Lagan Road,
Dublin/Ireland. Please use today's date and the notes given to you.

- information regarding immediate dispatch
- 100 pocket torches *Lightning* as per trial order WM/FC 4.5, collected this morning by
  forwarder GLX & Co.
- transport to airport Munich, airfreight via Frankfort to Dublin
- 1 case, marking WM/FC 4.5, gross weight 48 kilos,
- air waybill no. P-Z/F 259, copy attached
- hope that goods will arrive in perfect condition and sell well on home market
- look forward to receiving orders and expanding business relations.

8.1.2 Writing an advice of dispatch: E-mail / Letter Writing

Write an advice of despatch for your company K. Nakamoto Technologies, Fukuoka/Japan,
96 Hakataeki-Mei. Write this letter / Email by using today's date and the following notes.
Your customer is W. Schaller KG, Vienna/Austria, 24 Engerthstraße.

- refer to order AST/05 of 5th of last month
- machine parts ready for despatch, one week earlier than stated in order confirmation
- loading at Fukuoka port today, motor vessel Island Sun, shipping space booked
- cargo ship leaving tomorrow; according to shipping instructions dispatch to port
  Genoa/Italy, expected arrival 12th of next month, transshipment in Genoa,
  Multimodal Bill of Lading No. 547.25, 1 copy enclosed
- 2 cases, marked AST/05/1-2, 60 kilos each, containing machine parts for CNC machines
- transport from Genoa to Vienna by truck, Italian forwarder: Paolo Augustini & Co.,Genoa.
- positive ending of letter (free choice)

9. Transporting goods

When goods or services are ready for dispatch the question of how to send or transport the commodity must be answered. The answer to the problem is not that easy, because time, type of transport means, its speed and after all the transport costs, which might be rather high, must be considered. Just study the following comparison:

9.1 Comparing means of transport

Means of transport	Advantages	Disadvantages
by road: → lorries, trucks, vans	- vast road network - door-to-door service	- transport of bulk cargo - threat to environment
by rail: → cargo trains, freight trains	- many national and international freight depots - reasonable freight rates - different types of freight wagons - eco-friendly	- extra time and expenses for cartage to freight depots - careful packing may be essential
by air: → cargo planes, freight planes	- very fast and comfortable - not too many risks	- high freight rates - transport of relatively small quantities advisable - not environment-friendly
by sea: → cargo ships, freight ships, tankers, ferries, barges - ocean shipping - coastal shipping - domestic shipping - seaworthy packing may be needed	- used for bulky goods and huge quantities - favourable freight charges - ecological friendly	- rather slow - sea levels – high and low tide must be considered - important traffic links to ports, rivers, canals not available everywhere

9.1.1 Checklist on choosing suitable modes of transport

a. distance to the buyer, the sales market

b. quantity of goods to be delivered

c. weight of the consignment

d. freight charges, freight costs

e. type of goods: - solid, liquid, fragile, perishable, frozen goods,

                        - dangerous goods, e. g. flammable, toxic, radioactive material

                          and gases

                        - extremely valuable goods

                        - livestock

f. appropriate packing, e. g. seaworthy, waterproof, padded material, palette, foamed material, plastic foil,

g. means of transport with regard to safety and speed to avoid loss, damage or delay

h. access to transport facilities

i. availability of traffic links e. g. airports, harbours, road and rail networks, domestic waterways such as rivers and canals

9.1.2 Finding the right type of packaging

a. wooden cases	g. drums
b. crates	h. tins
c. card-board boxes	i. bales
d. bags and sacks	j. different pallet types
e. bottles	k. containers
f. barrels	l. igloos and cooling/refrigerated transport facilities

Task: How would you transport from Los Angeles:

a. to Mumbaj: 2 tons of scrap;   **f. to Madrid:** 80 chain saws;

b. to Vienna: 4 cases of machine parts;   **g. to Rome:** 150 loudspeakers;

c. to Chicago: 100 office chairs;   **h. to Helsinki:** bulky building material;

d. to Lagos: 1 parcel of hi-fi equipment;   **i. to Liverpool:** 400 kilos of fresh meat.

e: to Buenos Aires: 2 CDs containing new software;

9.2 Transport documents

Means of transport	Transport Documents needed
a. by road lorry, truck	**Road Consignment Note**
b. by rail cargo trains/freight trains	**Rail Consignment Note**
c. by sea MV motor vessels MS motor ships cargo ships / freight ships container ships tankers - **on inland waterways** barges	**Bill of Lading (B/L) / Ocean Bill of Lading** - **clean bill of lading** = goods loaded are in good order - **unclean/dirty/foul bill of lading** = the goods obviously are not in good order (e.g. damaged, broken, leaking) **Multimodal Bill of Lading** = different means of transport (plane, truck, train, ship) are used for one shipment **Domestic Inland Bill of Lading**: transport on rivers, canals, lakes
d. by air cargo planes / freight planes	**Air Waybill (AWB)**

9.3 Special export documentation

The following documents may be needed in export transactions:

a. Commercial invoice: Document made out by the exporter for his customer showing mainly the date and terms of sale, nature of goods, their quantity, unit and total price, taxes, weight of the shipment, etc. It is often required by customs authorities.

b. Customs invoice: Special type of invoice that is used to determine the real value of the imported goods.

c. Consular invoice: Special invoice legalized in the exporting country by the consul of the importing country to check imports and prevent over- and under-invoicing.

d. Insurance certificate: Document gives evidence that goods are insured against possible risks and certifies that an insurance policy has been bought.

e. Certificate of Origin: It certifies in which country the goods were produced and may influence the import duty that is charged according to different trade agreements among various nations.

f. Health certificate: All livestock must be accompanied by an official health certificate stating that the animals are healthy.

10. Dealing with complaints

10.1 Reasons for complaint

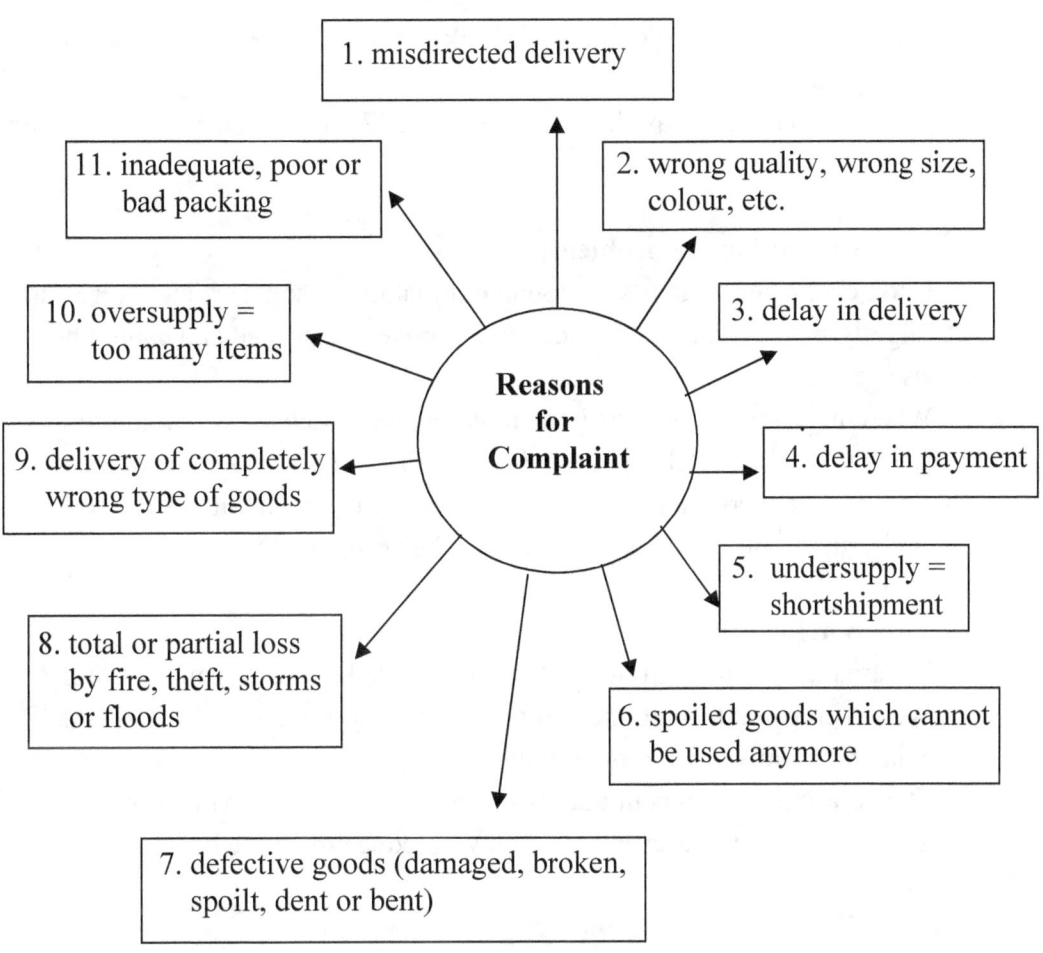

10.2 Solving complaints

a. placing the goods at the seller's disposal

b. asking for a replacement

c. getting a price reduction, discount, deduction

d. repairing the defective goods

e. supplying the right quantity, quality, size, colour, etc. without any delay

f. cancelling the sales contract and looking for another supplier

g. handing over the case to your solicitor/lawyer to take legal steps and go to court

Introduction:
- We are sorry to inform you that your consignment of last week has not met our expectations.
- We are writing to tell you that your delivery of 22 June has not come up to our approval.
- We regret having to say that our order no. 227/4 of March 15th has not turned out to our satisfaction.

Describing the problem
- Upon checking the goods we found out that many/some articles were partly/ slightly/badly/completely . . .damaged/broken/destroyed and cannot be used any more.
- When unpacking your consignment/cases, we noticed/saw that the following items were completely spoilt and can hardly be sold to our customers.
- Your last delivery of T-shirts has given cause for complaint as we noticed an undersupply of 80 items which cannot be accepted by us.

Solving the the problem
- We are placing the faulty/defective/misdirected goods at your disposal.
- We are prepared to keep the damaged/scratched/broken products/items if you grant/allow a 10 % price reduction.
- The poor /minor/deficient quality of the goods you sent with your last delivery can only be accepted when you reduce the price by 20 % .

Cause of the problem
- The damage may be due to rough handling in transit.
- The breakage must have happened during unloading the truck/container.
- The spoilage may be due to inadequate packing.
- The defect may have occurred through a mistake in your despatch department.

Requests
- We would appreciate your ideas what to do with the damaged goods.
- We would like to hear what to do with the defective items..
- Please let us have your replacement/replacement delivery as soon as possible.

Closing phrases
- We hope you will accommodate us and collect the goods within 2weeks/days.
- We trust you will sort out the problem soon.
- We ask you to settle this inconvenient matter without any delay.

10.3.1 Writing a letter of complaint: E-mail - Letter Writing

You are an employee in the purchasing department of Ramos Sanchez SL, 76 Avinguada Diagonal, 08019 Barcelona/Spain. Your supplier Ahmed Nadjib Textiles Ltd, 214 Nishtar Road, Karachi/Pakistan has delivered a consignment of sweaters which did not meet your approval. Your boss has asked you to write a letter of complaint by using the following notes. Please use today's date.

- confirm receipt of delivery by local haulage company Pedro Alvez today
- express that order no 838/CL has given cause for complaint
- state reasons as follows:
    - consignment delayed for more than one week
    - oversupply of 30 sweaters "fun", delivery note stated correct quantity
    - 40 sweaters "joy" wrong size XXL – sale difficult; correct size M
- place oversupply at supplier's disposal
- willing to keep sweaters in XXL at 20 % discount; in case supplier does not agree replacement as soon as possible, free of charge
- ask for immediate Email confirmation or phone call
- expect careful execution of future orders

10.3.2 Writing a letter of complaint: E-mail - Letter Writing

Write a letter of complaint to your supplier Swiss Watch S.A., 67 Rue de la Blanc, Geneve/ Switzerland. You work in the purchasing department of H. Matomela & Co., 47 Victoria Road, 8005 Cape Town/South Africa. Use today's date and the notes given to you.

- Your order 295/TC of 2nd of last month
- delivery yesterday by airfreight
- dissatisfied with delivery, second time within three weeks
- reasons:
    - you noticed poor packing
    - 40 alarm clocks badly damaged
    - 30 alarm clocks slightly scratched
- place badly damaged articles at seller's disposal, cannot be sold, photos enclosed
- agree to keep scratched items, ask for 20 % price reduction
- who is responsible for defective delivery?
- ask for further information how to carry on with problems
- improvements with deliveries important, otherwise no further orders.
- reply expected as soon as possible

Task - Matching exercise: Find out which of the following letters go together with the numbers of 10.1 (page 31)

a. The transport documents of the consignment the firm ABC received today showed that the real consignee was the company XYZ in Boston and not ABC.

b. Part of the shipment was lost in a heavy storm.

c. We hoped to get goods of first-class quality, but in fact received goods of inferior quality.

d. Upon checking the 4 cases, we noticed that half of the Barbie Dolls were damaged.

e. The packing list did not correspond to the number of items we got. Three alarm-clocks were missing.

f. Many of our customers do not pay their debts in time.

g. The promised delivery date concerning order no.3354/ST had not been kept by our supplier.

h. Instead of T-shirts our supplier in Thailand sent a delivery of finest silk underwear.

i. Although *HighTech plc* had only ordered 6 typewriters they got 8 of them.

j. *Icodo Ltd* complained that the computers from Taiwan were badly packed.

11. Warehousing

11.1 Main warehouse tasks

a. inspect and unpack incoming consignments

b. check stocks by permanent computerized stock control

c. protect goods from heat, water and keep them safe, clean and dry and avoid damage or loss

d. watch stock movements, stock turnover and update stock data

e. look after stock area and storage facilities such as multi-storey stocks, shelves cranes or fork-lift trucks and observe necessary safety rules

f. hand out working material to shop-floor workers

g. dispatch of goods to customers

h. returns to suppliers

i. streamline work with the purchasing department, production and the sales department

j. cooperate and discuss transport problems with forwarding agents

k. carrying out the company's permanent inventory

11.2 Warehouse sections

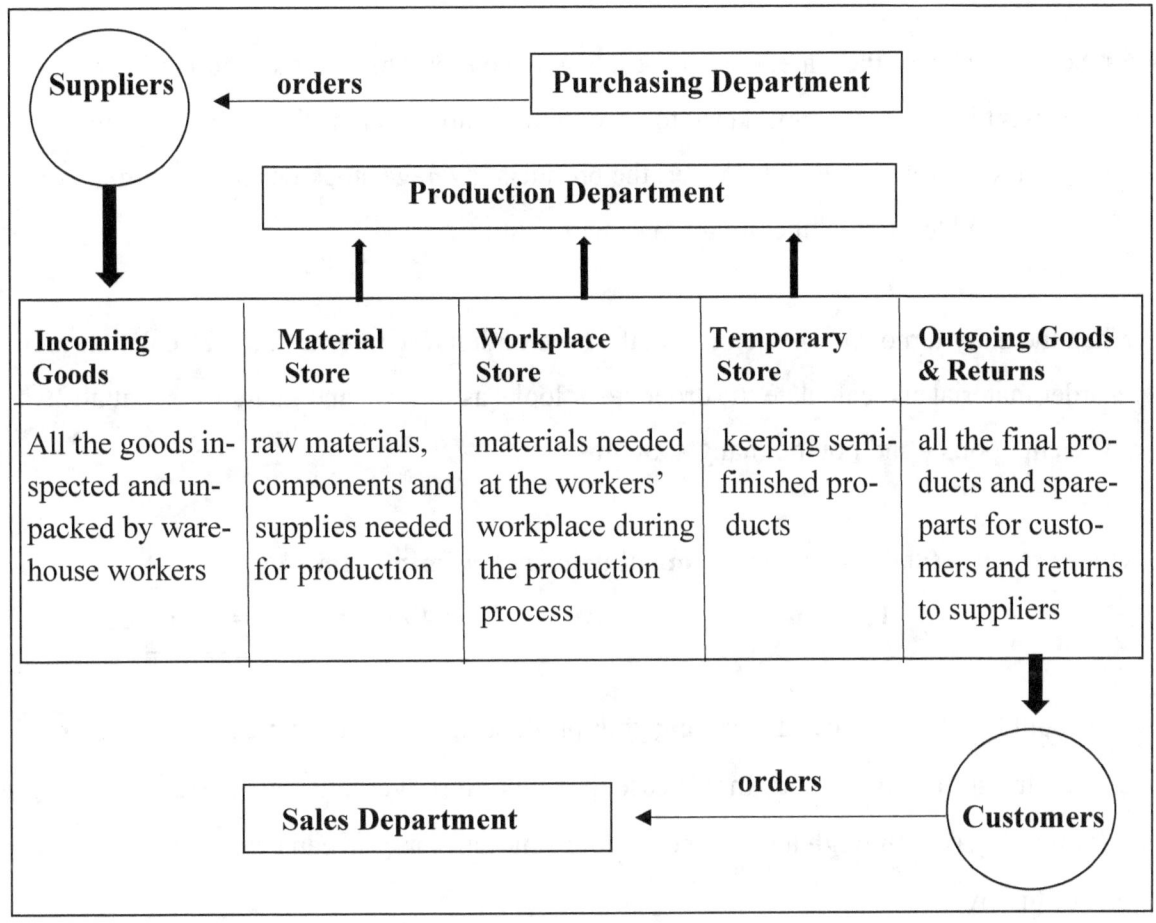

11.3 Warehouse-related costs

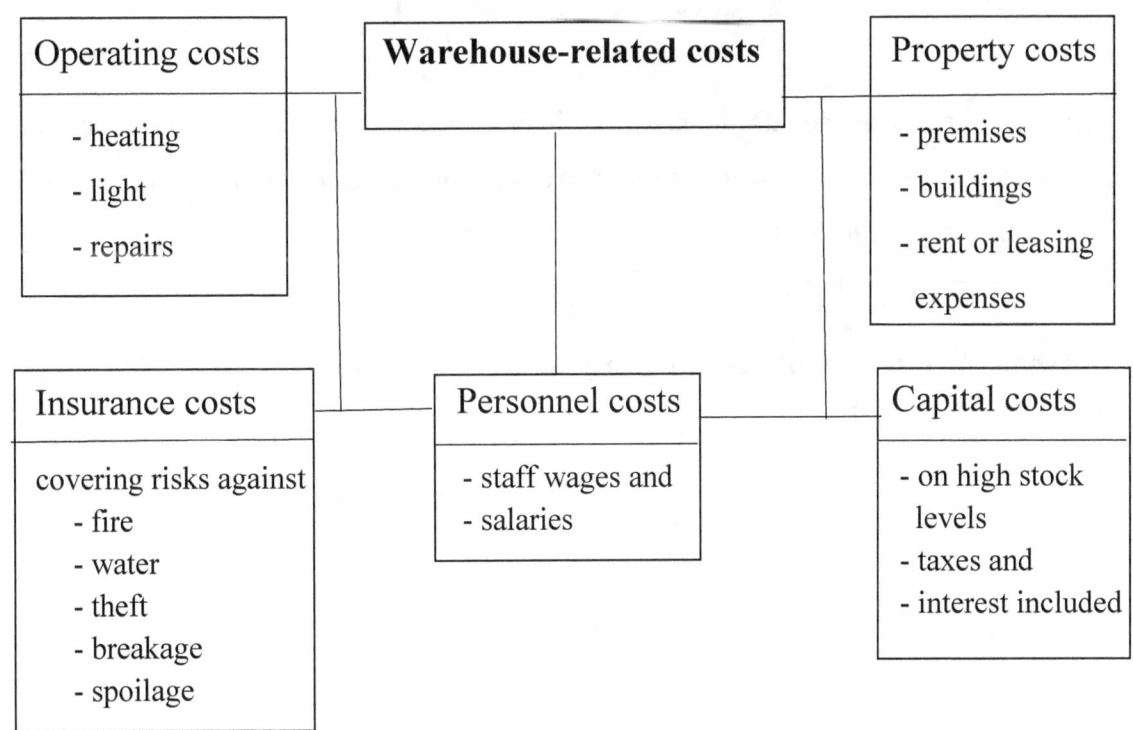

11.4 Fixing order quantities

As the total value of the warehouse materials may be pretty high and because of this too costly, it is of utmost importance to observe indicators such as the order stock, the average stock level, the stock turnover, the products' average stock period, the time of delivery and to find out the optimum order quantity.

When the daily turnover is 10 items and the time of delivery is 4 days, the calculation to re-order material and calculate the order stock looks as follows and guarantees that always sufficient goods – and not too many – are in stock:

Order stock = (daily turnover x time of delivery) + minimum stock

$$10 \text{ items} \quad \times \quad 4 \text{ days} \quad + \quad 40 \text{ items} \quad = 80 \text{ items}$$

You should also be interested in selling your products as fast as possible and as a result to keep the storage time short. In this case the rate of turnover must be considered. When a commodity runs through the warehouse four times a year, you can calculate its average rate of turnover.

Rate of turnover = 360 days : pace of turnover

$$360 \quad : \quad 4 \quad = \quad 90 \text{ days}$$

In particular as money counts, the inventory interest rate must be taken into consideration. If your stock level is too high you might be wasting capital and better take your money to your bank and get a surprising interest in return instead.

Warehousing rate or = interest rate per year x average rate of turnover : 360 days
Inventory interest rate

$$6 \% \quad \times \quad 90 \text{ days} \quad : \quad 360 \quad = 1,5 \%$$

12.1 Invoice essentials

1. Supplier's name and address
2. Customer's name and address
3. Invoice number and date
4. Order number and date
5. Article number
6. Description of the goods
7. Quantity of units sent

8. Unit price
9. Value/total price of items
10. Discounts
11. Insurance
12. Packing costs
13. Value Added Tax (VAT)
14. Total invoice amount

---

1. **Bikes & More Ltd.**

68 Kent Road   www.bikesmore.co.uk
Stafford   Phone: 0845 873 8440
Staffordshire
ST16 3HS
Great Britain

2. **Pro Bike & Co**
Bergstraße 46 - 48
CH-3005 B e r n
Switzerland

3. Invoice no.:   436/53
Date: December 12th 20 ..

4. Your order no.   493/St-K
Date: October 13th 20 . .

Pos.	Art.-no. 5.	Description 6.	Quantity 7.	£/Unit price 8.	Value 9.
1	7542.8	Mountainbikes „ Black Magic" frame size: 48 cm	30	145,60	4,368.00
2	3258.1	Mountainbike saddles "TOP"	20	12.60	252.00
					4,620.00
		10. Quantity discount 10 %			462.00
					4,158.00
		11. Insurance			130.20
		12. Packing costs			60,00
					4,348.20
		13. Value Added Tax 20 %			869.64
		14. Total Amount			5,217.84

12.2 Main types of invoices

a. Pro Forma Invoice

Detailed information is given about all the costs to be paid by the buyer before the goods are sent to him.

b. Commercial Invoice

Official invoice made out by the seller showing product details, prices, costs and deductions.

c. Consular Invoice

Invoice legalized in the exporting country by the consul of the importing country to check imports and prevent over- and under-invoicing and helps to get the real value of the goods imported by the buyer.

13. Non-payment and reminders

In this context reminders are not intended to remind people about meetings, seminars, marketing activities or very personal events. The sense of reminders discussed here is to remind business partners about invoices which had been due for payment for some time.

13.1 Types of reminders

a. First reminder = hidden reminder

It is often sent together with a sales letter, a circular or any advertising material and is written, more or less, friendly in tone.

b. Second reminder

This second letter is more demanding and less cordial than the first one. It appeals for cooperation and partnership and should convince the debtor to accept that there is no alternative to the win-win situation for both parties with regard to good business relations.

c. Third reminder

This or even one more collection letter might be written in case the two former reminders were not successful. Understandably, any of these final letters will be very strict and warn the debtor of the consequences in case he does not pay. If the debtor cannot give any really good reasons for non-payment, you will be able to take legal steps and go to court. Before doing so, you should state one fixed date/deadline and see if there is a happy ending after all.

13.2 Communication concerning reminders

Hidden Reminder:
- As you are always interested in getting our special offers, please find enclosed leaflets showing some models of our new summer collection. At the same time we are sorry to inform you that our invoice no. 2319/CY of Nov. 14th for € 1,400, 60 is overdue for more than ten days now and kindly ask you to settle your account soon.

First Reminder:
- We regret having to say that our invoice no. 987/4 of March 15 for $ 950,10 was due for payment last week. We look forward to receiving your remittance within the next few days.
- As it may have escaped your notice, we would like to remind you of the outstanding amount of our last invoice which you may have overlooked and ask you to transfer the balance of ¥ 680.80 without any further delay.

Second Reminder:
- We are writing to tell you that we have not received any reply to our letter dated 4 of August regarding the overdue amount of £ 574.30 and ask you to transfer the open amount to our bank account by return or to give reasons for the delay in payment.
- We are sorry to say that you have neither answered our last letter nor cleared your account. We now expect you to clear the outstanding balance of CAN $ 1,400.-- immediately.

Third Reminder:
- As you have disregarded all our letters concerning invoice no. 56/P dated 16 May and to remit the outstanding amount of € 2,270.--, we are forced to state May 30th as the final date for payment. If you should fail to meet this deadline, we will be forced to start legal steps to recover the overdue amount.
- We must now insist on settling your account by April 20 at the latest. If you should fail to pay, the case will be handed over to our solicitors in order to start legal proceedings against you.

Closing phrases:
- If you should have arranged payment meanwhile, please ignore this letter and accept our thanks.
- We would be grateful to receive your payment soon and look forward to settling this inconvenient matter.
- We are not prepared to postpone payment to settle your account any longer and hope that you will accommodate us and remit the open amount without any further delay. In case you do not pay immediately, extra charges for late payment will be imposed.
- As we have been waiting for your remittance for such a long time, we cannot grant you any extension for payment now.

13.3 Communication and reply to reminders

Introduction and apology

- Much to our regret, we have overlooked your invoice no. AX/16 dated 20th of February and have transferred the open sum, as requested, today.
- We are very sorry for the delay in payment and have instructed our bank to remit the outstanding balance to your account at the ABC bank this morning.
- We sincerely apologise for this unpleasant incident and assure you to make payment of the amount in question immediately.

Unjustified request for payment

- With reference to your letter of 25 of March requesting the outstanding amount of $ 470.30 we ask you to check your books to see that this particular sum of money was paid without any delay.
- We thank you for your letter dated 25 of March and are sorry to say that an oversight has obviously occurred in your Accounts Department. In fact, the invoice amount was transferred to your bank account on time.

Stating reasons for non-payment

- We were unable to settle our account because two of our major customers went bankrupt.
- Due to the weak economic situation, the world-wide slump and global financial crisis we had not been able to remit the outstanding invoice amount of $ 470.30 punctually.
- Payment has not been made to you because our own customers are having problems to meet their obligations as agreed and to settle their outstanding accounts without any delay.

Requests to solve problem

- We ask you to extend the deadline for payment by 8 days/one month.
- We would be grateful if you could accommodate us and grant us an extension of 2 weeks.
- With reference to the problems described, we ask you either to postpone payment or should appreciate to pay the total sum in two instalments.

Closing phrases

- We hope that our long-standing business relations will not be affected by this inconvenient matter and look forward to hearing from you soon.
- We trust that you will understand our predicament and assist us in this matter in order to continue our cooperation in future times.

13.3.1 Writing a first/hidden reminder: E-mail / Letter Writing

Write two reminders for your employer James Brown & Co., 216 High Gate, 10018 New York to your debtor Marcel Miraux & Fils, 89 Rue de Liège, 1070 Brussels/Belgium. Please use today's date and the following notes on the reminders and the reply:

- enclose circular to inform about product improvements
  - characteristics of new *TTS* motors:
    more powerful, first-class quality, higher safety standards, reduced price
  - more efficient than competing products, shown in tests
  - refer to: invoice no. AX/16, invoice date 20th February, invoice amount $ 470.30, due for payment last week
- possible oversight of invoice in question
- payment expected next few days

13.3.2 Writing a third/last reminder: E-mail / Letter Writing

- no reply to all your letters asking for payment
- last reference made to invoice no. AX/16, amount $ 470.30, account not settled
- final date for payment 20 of this month
- if deadline is disregarded, lawyers in legal department will take legal steps to recover balance still outstanding
- hope of understanding, but you are reluctant to wait any longer and cannot grant any further extension for payment

13.3.3 Writing a reply to reminder: E-mail / Letter Writing

- feel very sorry for non-payment of invoice no. 231/FK dated 28th June
- not able to settle sum of € 3,865.80 due on 28th July
- refer to:
  - global economic problems
  - bankruptcy of customer
  - payments made sluggishly
- ask for extension of deadline by 4 weeks
- be prepared to make part-payment of € 2,000,-- within next 2 weeks at the latest
- payment of rest punctually
- trust to find understanding for predicament and willingness to help in particular situation
- look forward to hearing from creditor soon.

14 Global business

14.1 Export risks

Over the last few decades world trade and international business relations have developed extremely well and pushed the trade of any kind of merchandise and commercial services such as telecommunications, finance, insurance, transport and travel. The number of global players has grown steadily and their main global objectives and reasons to internationalize look quite similar. They may take the initiative themselves, be encouraged by global politics or they are simply forced by competition.

In any case, however, the decision towards globalization must be taken carefully in order to avoid a flop and waste of money.

Potential exporters planning to expand business should consider the following main risks when selling their products abroad:

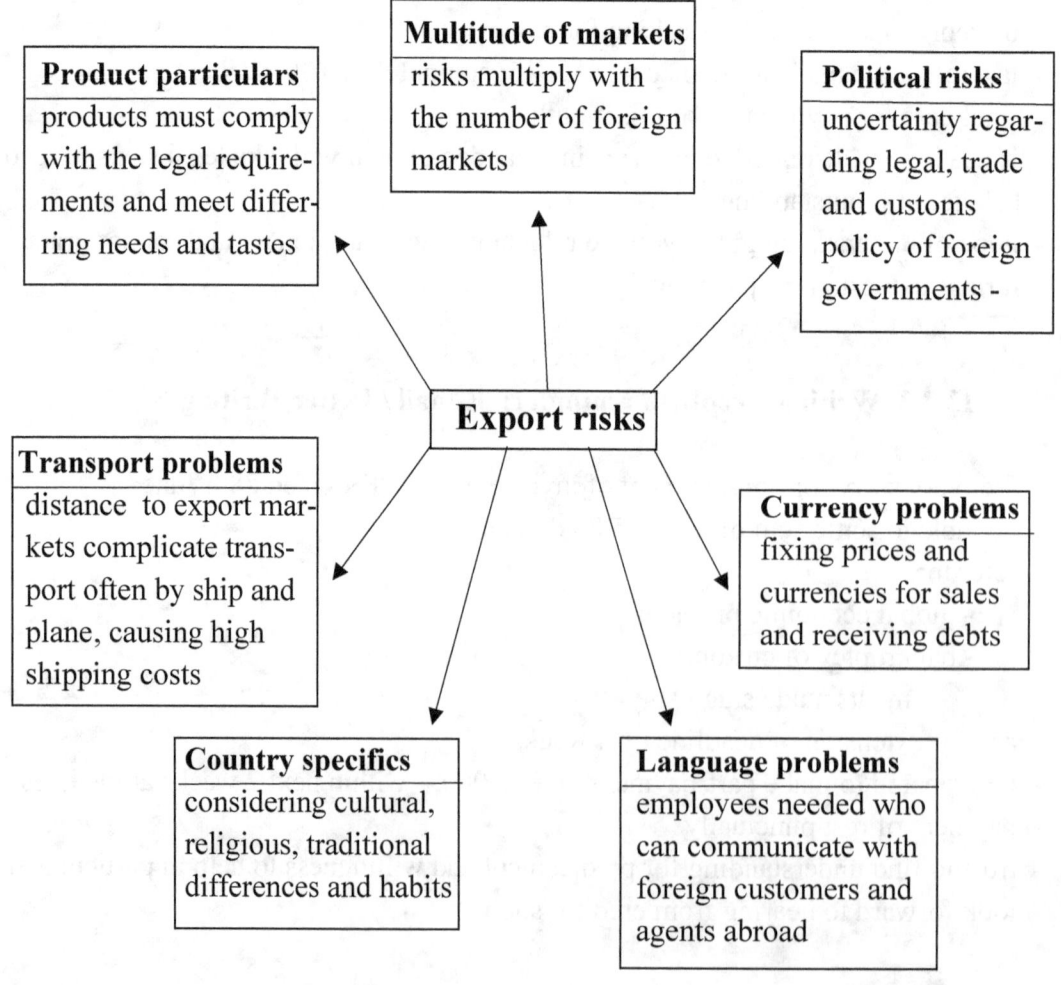

14.2 Foreign direct investments and international partnerships

Despite the risks described before, the interest in investing capital abroad and and doing business with foreign partners has not declined. The latest statistics concerning **Foreign Direct Investments (FDI)** clearly proves the upward trend towards any form of globalization. Cross-border investments are mainly done by industrialised countries, particularly by EU countries, the USA, China and Japan. Manufacturing industries such as the automobile, textile, computer and electrical industries benefitted from foreign direct investments in the same way as transport, storage, finance and insurance did in the wide field of the service sector.

In most cases enterprises carefully promote their global expansion by establishing international partnerships. They share common efforts and risks and benefit from all the positive effects their investment might have.

The business partners Mid-West Ltd and Hobson & Co decided to start an advertising campaign for their products in China together. As there was a booming market, promising sales were pretty sure. They agreed to set up a factory and use the same trade channels to market their products. After very successful years the more powerful Mid-West Ltd took over its smaller partner Hobson & Co. That is the way business often goes and is taken in the following three steps:

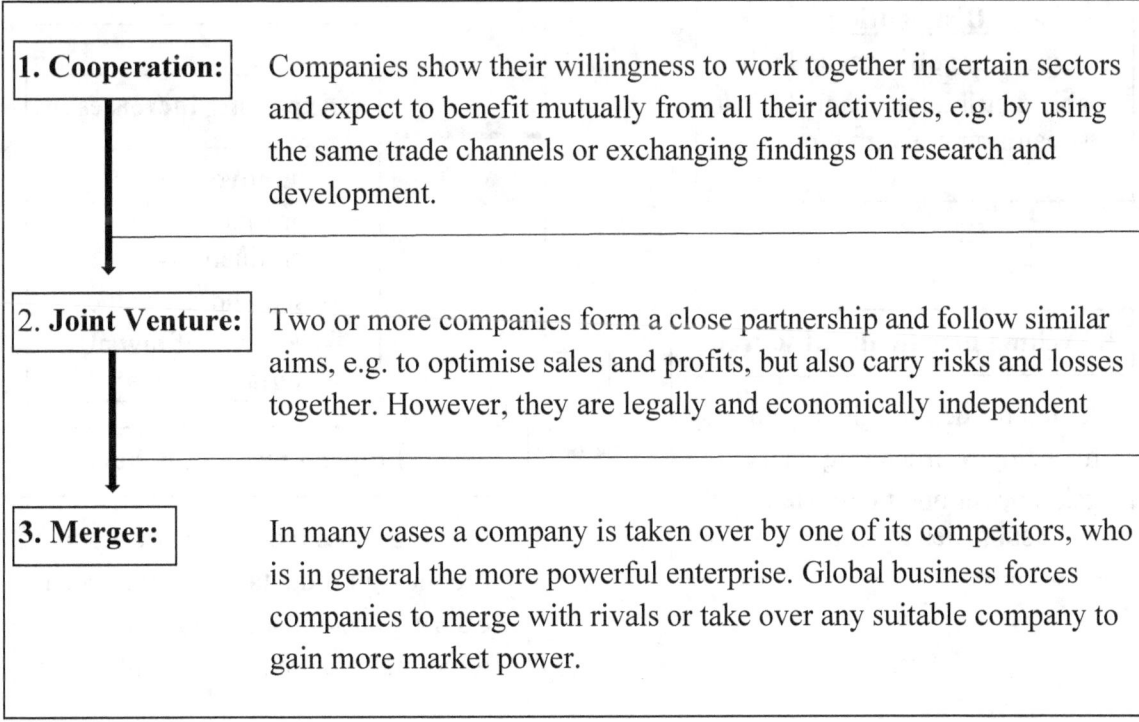

1. Cooperation: Companies show their willingness to work together in certain sectors and expect to benefit mutually from all their activities, e.g. by using the same trade channels or exchanging findings on research and development.

2. Joint Venture: Two or more companies form a close partnership and follow similar aims, e.g. to optimise sales and profits, but also carry risks and losses together. However, they are legally and economically independent

3. Merger: In many cases a company is taken over by one of its competitors, who is in general the more powerful enterprise. Global business forces companies to merge with rivals or take over any suitable company to gain more market power.

14.3 Objectives of mergers

In order to improve the company's key figures and be more efficient just "leaner" the main reasons and expectations of globalisation are as follows:

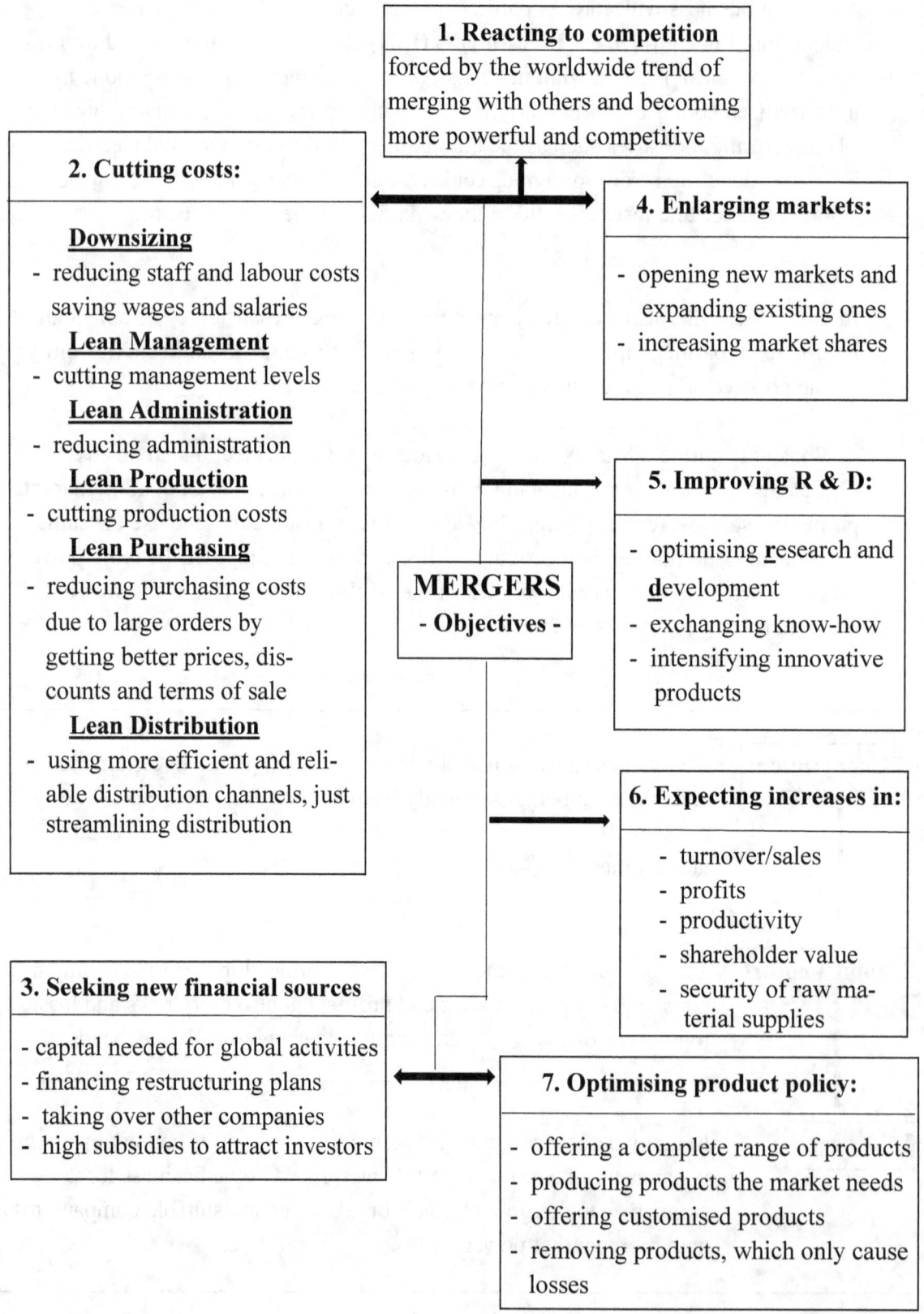

1. Reacting to competition

forced by the worldwide trend of merging with others and becoming more powerful and competitive

2. Cutting costs:

Downsizing
- reducing staff and labour costs saving wages and salaries

Lean Management
- cutting management levels

Lean Administration
- reducing administration

Lean Production
- cutting production costs

Lean Purchasing
- reducing purchasing costs due to large orders by getting better prices, discounts and terms of sale

Lean Distribution
- using more efficient and reliable distribution channels, just streamlining distribution

4. Enlarging markets:

- opening new markets and expanding existing ones
- increasing market shares

**MERGERS
- Objectives -**

5. Improving R & D:

- optimising research and development
- exchanging know-how
- intensifying innovative products

6. Expecting increases in:

- turnover/sales
- profits
- productivity
- shareholder value
- security of raw material supplies

3. Seeking new financial sources

- capital needed for global activities
- financing restructuring plans
- taking over other companies
- high subsidies to attract investors

7. Optimising product policy:

- offering a complete range of products
- producing products the market needs
- offering customised products
- removing products, which only cause losses

15.1 Working conditions

The contract of employment stipulates in detail the staff's working conditions. In general, the main points of paid work and employment relationships as well as factors which influence the employees' well-being at work looks as follows and may become a win-win situation for employers and their employees:

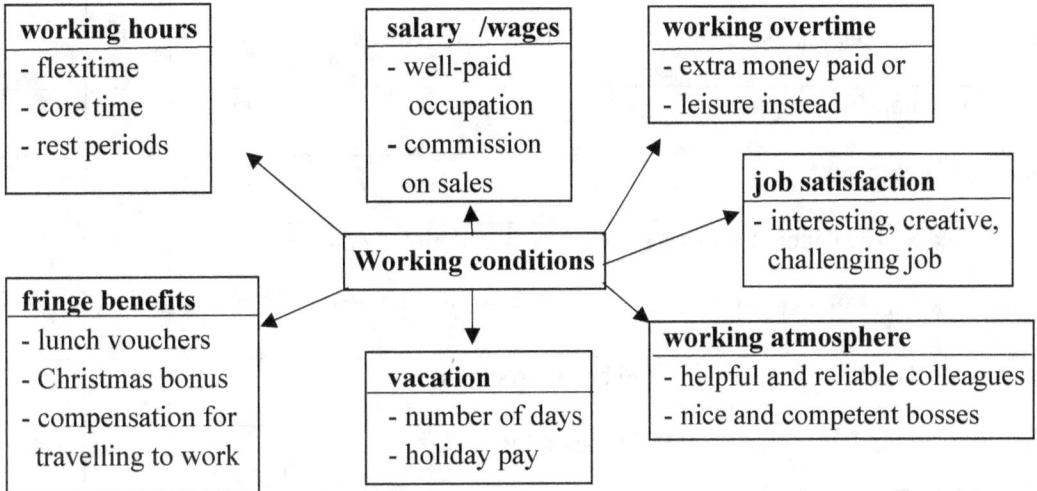

15.2 Soft skills and core competences

When starting working life in business two very important competences are expected by your employer. It is needless to say that your hard skills are essential and consist of your professional qualifications, degrees and certificates which certify in detail the job applicant's qualifications.

Apart from this, the following, non-exhaustive enumeration of soft skills refers to core competences which are of prior importance today in application procedures and thus may facilitate your life as a smart workmate at your place of work.

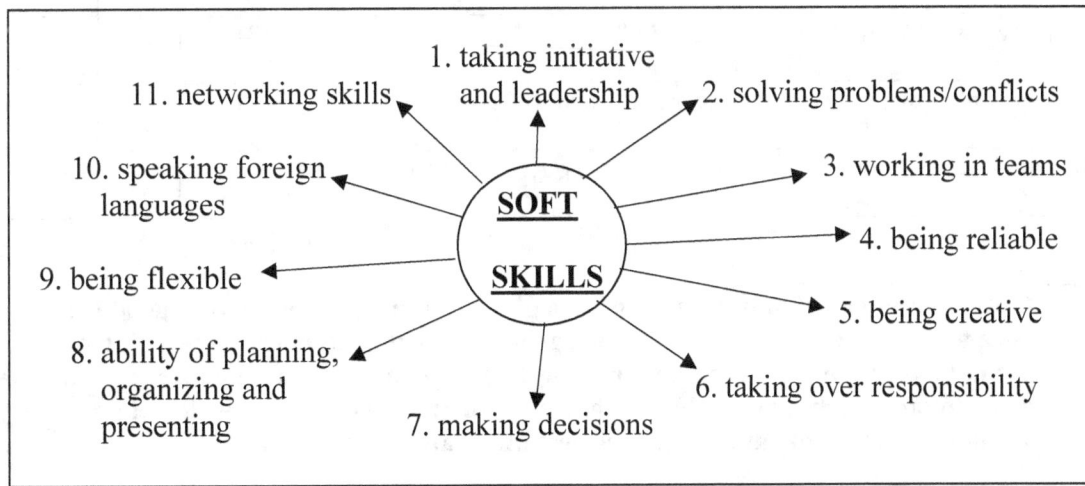

Game to test yourself, workmates, friends. If so write down their scores and names.

	Ask yourself or anybody else you like	max.	Scores yours	workmate
	WHO ...???			
1.	knows the world's 5 leading trading nations	(5)		
2.	can describe 5 important soft skills	(5)		
3.	can give 3 international stock markets and their share indices	(6)		
4.	can state 5 non-EU currencies	(5)		
5.	knows 5 **Incoterms**	(5)		
6.	can state a Swiss, Dutch, Chinese, Korean, Japanese global company	(5)		
7.	can give 3 international airlines	(3)		
8.	knows the difference between job and batch production	(2)		
9.	knows what the English term „**IMF**" stands for	(2)		
10.	can describe 4 export risks	(4)		
11.	knows 3 important export sectors of your economy	(3)		
12.	can explain what a „joint venture" is	(2)		
13.	knows what a **Certificate of Origin** is and **who issues** it	(4)		
14.	knows the documents used for the transport by road and ship	(4)		
15.	can give 1 secure method of payment used in international business	(2)		
16.	can state 5 essentials an offer should contain	(5)		
17.	knows the difference between a merger and a takeover	(2)		
18.	knows what kind of person a „**C.E.O.**" is	(2)		
19.	can explain what **AWB** stands for and when it is used	(2)		
20.	can describe 2 Ps of marketing and what the AIDA formula consists of	(6)		
		(74)		

Results:
**74 – 68 pts = great global player and expert in globalisation; 67 – 60 = very good career prospects / branch manager; 59 – 50 = well done, good workmate, but carry on working hard;
49 – 37 = not too bad, but could be better – don't give up improving economics; 36 – 22 pts = go back to school/university again to learn what is missing; 21 pts and less = hopeless case – you should look for another job and forget business life at all (sorry, just a joke!)**